RADICALLY

Alive

BEYOND ABUSE

Gillian,

Live Radically Alive!

Choose You!

LIVE Your ROAR!

♡

RADICALLY *Alive*

BEYOND ABUSE

DR. LISA COONEY

Acknowledgements

I am in deep gratitude to:

Gigi, Donna, Ramona, Mathes, Sage, Mandi, Laura, Tara, Linda, Reid, Krista, Jen, Megan, Sage, Anna Lena, Rebecca, Linda and the other countless consciousness seekers who have worked tirelessly behind the scenes who led the way in this creation by handling all the logistics so I could travel and bring Radical Aliveness to those who have and are still struggling with moving beyond the past and abuse.

Erica Glessing, CEO of Happy Publishing, for reaching out and acknowledging my brilliance and instigating eight number 1 international bestsellers that has led to a big exposure professionally and beyond. Thank you Happy Publishing for granting full rights for inclusion in this book any content that ran in other Happy Publishing books.

Gary Douglas and Dr. Dain Heer and the tools of Access Consciousness®. I was so lost when I found you. The death of a parent propelled me to seek something completely different. What I found beneath the layers of trauma and abuse, by BOTH your skilled guidance, kindness and expertise was ME. What you both be and do is an inspiration and a gift. Thank you.

Sandra Rogers, the Executive Producer of my Voice America Empowerment Radio Show, and Voice America for seeking me out and putting me on the air. My passion to rid the world of abuse and empower all people to live Radically Alive was magnified through this show.

My voice is now heard and has the potential to be heard all around the world in every country or city with internet. No matter where someone is, and if they are struggling with how to move beyond abuse, and create a life of radical aliveness they can hear the show and read this book.

And there is so much more to come...

Introduction

Over the past 20 years, I've committed my life to helping others get free from the 'prison of abuse' and create a meaningful and joyful life for themselves. I've worked with thousands of clients who rave about the brilliant results they've achieved through the type of facilitation I offer them – one that is balanced with potency, sexual-ness (the energy of receiving) and vulnerability.

In this book, you'll get a glimpse into this work which allows you to not only overcome an abusive past, but propels you beyond anything that has stopped you from full out living thus far.

As a trained psychotherapist, I spent most of my early career following a traditional path of thought as to how might people heal from trauma and abuse. And it probably would have continued if I hadn't been my own best student.

You could say everything I've learned has been won the hard way–by experiencing it.

Let me explain…

For the first two decades of my life I was extremely unhappy. In my early 20s, I tried to numb out by drinking, using drugs, and partying. I was overweight and didn't care about myself.

One night I almost died because of my reckless behavior.

You see, I grew up in a very violent household. I was abused sexually, physically, and emotionally from the time I was a baby into my 20s.

I felt guilty, helpless, and in terror all the time. Nothing I did seemed to help and happiness was hopelessly out of reach. It seemed impossible to me to even live. The abuse had control over every aspect of my life.

Everything felt wrong, including me.

I never felt like I fit in anywhere. The only thing that made me happy was alcohol and escaping. I would drink or snort anything I could get my hands on in order to not feel anything. It felt like the best way to exist: dazed and confused.

When I got to college, I walked around campus with my eyes down and shoulders hunched. One day, a professor reached out to me and asked me if I was all right. Nobody had ever asked me this before. Ever. My eyes immediately filled with tears.

She helped me realize that what I'd been living with was treatable, and filled me with hope that I could get beyond this and create a new life for myself. And that's what I've done.

Today, I'm living my dream life beyond anything I ever imagined: I travel for work and pleasure internationally, facilitating classes on being Radically Alive Beyond Abuse and Receiving Energy with our bodies. I live in a beautiful home that I share with someone I adore. I am surrounded by 25 acres of beautiful earth, 20 horses, 3 dogs, and so much more. I have intimate, nurturing and supportive relationships with friends and loved ones. I am vibrant and always choosing more.

No matter what my trauma and past tragedy has been, I am vigilant about making choices beyond it. I'm happy – the happiest I've ever been with me. I have finally 'received' me and I keep on learning new ways to do so.

Abuse Knows No Boundaries

Abuse, by its very nature, covers a broad territory.

It happens to us and *it happens within us* – and perpetuates itself throughout all the nooks and crannies of our experience.

It shows up in the ways you think, talk, act – and don't act.

It shows up in your finances, your capacity for earning money, the kinds of jobs or work you choose.

It shows up in every relationship you have – from the neighbor down the street, the friends you keep, or the partner you commit to.

Or don't commit to.

It shows up in your health, the way your body looks and functions, the foods you eat.

And I could go on...

It doesn't matter where you see your experience landing on the continuum of abuse. The important thing is to acknowledge and challenge these experiences. Maybe you lived through early childhood abuse like the trauma and horror that I did. Or maybe your parents divorced when you were young and you never saw your dad (or mom) again. Maybe your parents fought about money and today you struggle to make a living.

Whatever the range or breadth of it... it's all welcome here.

We live in an inclusive Universe.

Breaking Out and into Freedom

What would it be like for you to live beyond your current experience? What dreams do you hold in your heart? What whisperings of consciousness do you hear?

Maybe you know and maybe you don't. Not everyone who comes to me starts out knowing what they want on a conscious level. Years of denial and judgement and abuse exacts a high price in the cost of living, and sometimes all you have left to show for it is a small morsel of life, barely surviving.

This book will show you how to break free of something I call the 'invisible cage of abuse.'

It will open you to new ideas about what's possible and give you concepts you can engage with at any place you find yourself any time. And it doesn't matter whether you have a history of past abuse or not because these principles and tips will work for anyone.

On the other hand, if you do have an abusive past, it may well be a lifeline.

One note: If you find that some of these concepts – and the language – I use is new to you, that's a good thing. No, it's not a typo, but a specific way of saying something that's rooted in certain modalities I use. Because, even though I'm a licensed psychotherapist, I've also been trained and certified in many kinds of alternative healing therapies, so sometimes my choice of words comes from those. (If you want to learn more, please visit my website at www.DrLisaCooney.com.)

One thing's for certain...

If you put into practice the material you read here, you *will* get unstuck from whatever is plaguing you or preventing you from choosing what you would like to create.

This will move you in the direction of what I call *Radical Aliveness*...and I can't wait to share it with you.

Let's get started!

Dedication

This book is dedicated to you, the reader, thank you for choosing a new possibility for you. Thank you for choosing to get free of your past. Thank you for knowing that no matter what your tragedy, trauma or limitation may be or have been, you are a powerful and potent creator of magnitude and you can always choose beyond your circumstance.

If you are anything like me you may at one time or many times fallen ill to the dis-ease of depression, illness, lack and loneliness. I found these tools and words presented in this book significantly aided me in my recovery to reclaim the fullest and freest expression of me. I attempted simple and pragmatic here. I hope you find them useful to you as well.

I know with trauma and abuse, things aren't so simple and overwhelm is prominent. May you find peace and even solace knowing that as long as you never give up, never give in and never quit these words can work for you too.

May you be inspired and may your traumatic transform to Radically Alive Beyond Abuse.

My friend always:

Choose YOU

Commit to YOU

Collaborate with the Universe Conspiring to Bless YOU

and Create for and with YOU

TABLE OF CONTENTS

One

MOVING BEYOND THE INVISIBLE CAGE OF ABUSE

Moving on is a simple thing. What it leaves behind, is hard.
~ Dave Mustaine

"Can you give me the details of your early childhood abuse?"

There was a long silence after my editor asked me this question. She had recently reviewed the first draft of my book, *Kick Abuse in the Caboose*, and wanted to fill in more details of my past abuse. I asked her to give me a moment so I could recall everything.

A full eight minutes later, I began listing the details to her.

During those eight minutes, I scanned my body and was amazed to discover that the two decades of physical, sexual, emotional, financial, spiritual and physiological abuse I had experienced no longer 'inhabited' my body – although I could remember the heaviness of all the perpetration.

As I shared the details with her, I felt as if I was sharing a client's or a friend's story, not mine. I wasn't dissociating or disconnecting; rather, I had embodied me beyond my story of abuse.

I smiled as I realized just how far I had come in my journey of moving beyond abuse.

One of the things that helped me immensely was reading self-help books – like you're doing now – highlighting sentences until the words leapt off the page and entered me, giving me a glimpse of a different reality. Knowing that others understood what I was experiencing gave me hope.

And I discovered I certainly wasn't alone.

I did other things, too. For example, I tried to hike, meditate, swim and bike the abuse out of me. I sought counseling, and even earned a Master's degree and a Doctorate in Psychology myself. I was committed to continually educating myself clinically, energetically and psychologically, determined to find a way to move beyond abuse.

As I facilitated workshop after workshop and freed others from their abuse, ultimately, I freed myself as well. And I haven't stopped. My commitment continues to be to eradicate and eliminate abuse in all its many forms from this planet through the Live Your ROAR movement.

MOVING BEYOND ABUSE: A NEW PARADIGM OF HEALING

Perhaps you've experienced abuse, whether sexual, physical, spiritual, financial or emotional. It may have been a single event or a series of incidents.

You may have already invested a vast amount of time and energy in healing your experience of abuse and, perhaps, not seen the results you desired. That's understandable. Unfortunately, I've found that a lot of tools and practices that preceded the approach I take to moving beyond abuse are about fixing ourselves and defining ourselves by our story of abuse.

I am not of the belief that we must fix ourselves in order to be free. When we adopt this model, we assume that there's something wrong with us and we look for solutions to fix the problem. It becomes a bottomless pit. And we never get to the end of it because we never feel fixed or whole. Instead, you find yourself going around in similar circles, wondering if it will ever end, waiting for the day when you are finally healed. Healing abuse does occur in layers, cometimes many layers, focusing on what's right about you is the cornerstone to empowering yourself beyond abuse.

This chapter, some of which is excerpted from my forthcoming book, *Kick Abuse in the Caboose*, describes a new way of healing beyond abuse.

You're going to discover that you don't need to fix anything or remain defined by your abuse. You'll also discover how to make the choice of ending perpetration and no longer allowing that one act or series of events to dominate your entire life.

THE INVISIBLE CAGE OF ABUSE

I spent much of my life in an invisible cage.

I say it was invisible because although I lived inside it, a silent prisoner, I wasn't even aware that it existed. It took me decades to name it, let alone to shape it into a message that I could share with the world. Yet every time I talk about the invisible cage to someone who has experienced abuse, a look of recognition, often relief, sweeps across their face. You may be having a similar experience yourself right now as you read these words.

The cage includes a subtle judgement about the wrongness of you that you take for granted to be true. In other words, you perceive yourself to be bad or wrong because of the abuse that occurred. This "wrongness" becomes the filter through which you experience and perceive reality. As a result, you create your life *from* the perpetration and imprison yourself within it.

Your cage is like a ghost that continuously whispers in your ear. It whispers when you have challenges. Even when life is good, it doesn't stop. In fact, at these times it's likely to get louder with a desperate attempt to keep you inside the cage of abuse. Living within the limits of the cage keeps you held in a place that's familiar. There's a strange comfort in the confines of the cage, however much you desire to live beyond it.

The cage is based on lack, limitation and lie.

The cage keeps you out of freedom, pleasure and possibility.

To live inside the cage is to live without a voice. You may be able to speak and function in the world, but there remains a part of you isolated, silenced and cut off from reality – a part that lives inside you, deadened and numbed out.

The pain of living inside the cage can be so great that sometimes you choose not to dwell there at all. You may numb out or check out to avoid the pain. You might do this periodically throughout the day, checking out of your body. You may also use food, alcohol, drugs or medication to check out more deeply.

You become a shell of who you truly are.

You wonder why you're 'self-sabotaging', when what you're actually doing is operating from what the cage is designed to do: fight life and say 'no' from a place of contraction rather than embrace life and say 'yes' from a place of expansion. Inside the cage, you continue to react to life from the patterns of past abuse and this keeps the perpetration alive.

You may have also noticed that when you live from within the cage of abuse, it reverberates through all other areas of your life. When you're filtering the world through the lens of abuse, it's as though more of it gets drawn to you, leading to more self-blame. And phrases such as, "You create your own reality," don't help. When the pattern of abuse continuously perpetuates itself and you don't know how to stop it, it adds to the feeling that there's something wrong with you.

What often happens from within the cage is that, because abuse mires our reality, our perception gets twisted into a mild form of insanity. What seems true can be false and vice versa. We find ourselves trusting people who shouldn't be trusted, and not trusting people who we could. People may come into our lives who represent all the things we've been saying we want to generate and manifest, but we push them away because to engage with them would mean living beyond the cage and we feel uncomfortable doing so.

If you've been walking around in the invisible cage of abuse, you've probably assumed that this was your only choice. In fact, for most people that I've worked with, the idea of choice at first seems confusing. We have been sold the myth that, because we've experienced abuse, our lives will be forever filled with suffering. Your life, up until now, has possibly provided you with plenty of evidence that this is the case.

Yet living in the invisible cage of abuse as a silent prisoner is not your only choice.

Make Friends with The Cage of Abuse

What I've discovered in supporting tens of thousands of people around the world to overcome abuse is that we don't necessarily make our way out of the cage by a quick fix.

First, we must increase our awareness and acknowledge the cage.

This moment you may be waking up for the first time to understanding that the cage exists. People often say, "Oh, that's what it is," when they hear me talk about the cage, giving words to something that usually remains unnamed.

It's like there's been an elephant shitting in the room all along and everyone was silently stepping around it. We're no longer ignoring it. It stinks, and now we're dealing with it.

After you acknowledge the cage, you get to accept that you've been living in it. In a very real sense, the cage has actually been your biggest ally in healing: *it protected you during a time you needed protection.*

The beauty is that, when you embrace the cage while also choosing something other than shutting down, you soften. You open to the possibility of being in communion with your pain. Ultimately, this is the only way to dissolve the bars of the cage and step into the true freedom, joy and possibility that exists independent of it.

In order to step out of the cage, you don't actually have to get anything 'back.' This is where my approach differs radically from what you may have experienced before in other kinds of therapies. Instead, you learn how to make different kinds of choices that don't perpetuate the abuse. You discover how to connect with yourself beyond the insanity that created the cage in the first place. And you choose to live without making what happened to you (whether it was a single act or a series of events) into your entire life.

It's likely that your whole reality will begin to shift as you start to notice how the invisible cage shows up in your own life.

MOVING BEYOND THE CAGE OF ABUSE

The cruel joke about abuse is that it ended a long time ago, yet you keep it going by treating yourself like the abuser treated you.

Why do you do this?

The invisible cage of abuse holds you prisoner to the belief that you are somehow wrong or bad; that you don't deserve to live for yourself

20

but rather need to do what others think you should do, or what you're supposed to do (just like what happened during your abuse: you did what you were told and your needs didn't matter).

When you make friends with the cage of abuse, you stop being at war with yourself. This is the place from which you start choosing you and committing to your own life.

What does this look like?

Committing to your life looks like standing up for what you choose no matter what happens. It's never giving in and never giving up (says the Irish Fighter in me). And yet it's not about *pushing, efforting, excluding or fighting.*

You no longer need to prove or fight to have your life for yourself. You simply get to choose it. This commitment to life is not heavy – it's actually the ease, lightness, joy and fun that's possible when you choose for you. And it actually requires a kindness with yourself that you may never have experienced before.

But there's a bigger block you may run into in committing to your life...

I've guided thousands of people to overcome their sexual abuse and one of the biggest challenges I see them struggle with is letting go of their story of abuse. It's their story, and the role of victim within their story, that keeps them from committing to themselves. It's like they were more committed to the story of abuse rather than the possibility of life beyond it. I've been there myself. I know this. Yet it only needs to be a "phase" in your journey from the cage of abuse to radical aliveness.

When you hold onto the story of abuse you keep yourself trapped in the role of "victim." It seems like "life happens" to you; that you're a victim of circumstance; that no matter what you do you're going to get f*cked, anyway, so why bother?

Abuse, then, becomes a great excuse for not committing to your own life.

But there's another possibility I'd like to show you.

When you put down the story of abuse, get support to release all the inner anguish about your abuse, and move out of the cage of abuse and the wrongness of you, a space opens up for something new:

You discover the 'phenomenance' of you.

You become *radically alive* – a space of being where the abuse no longer runs your life and you are generating and creating a life for yourself far beyond anything you could have ever imagined.

In the next chapter, you'll learn more about this cage of abuse and its impact on your natural ability to create.

Two

Creativity as the Space of Possibility

I dwell in possibility.
~ Emily Dickinson

Abuse is one of the biggest obstacles to creativity.

Actually, if the truth be told, it's not the abuse itself because, in most cases, by the time my clients come to see me, the abuse has ended. It may have been an isolated incident in their past or many experiences of abuse over decades.

Either way, the feeling people describe is 'stuckness.' It's as though they're trapped in an invisible cage, some kind of destructive force that blocks them from fully creating their life.

So, really, it's the *cage of abuse* that's one of the biggest obstacles to creativity. The cage of abuse perpetuates destruction, withdrawal, separation and isolation and, when you're locked in it, you're in a constant state of degrading and disempowering yourself.

The Invisible Cage of Abuse

If you've ever experienced abuse, it's easy to get stuck in repeating patterns of that past abuse that show up as limitation around your health, relationships and money flows.

Essentially, your generative and creative capacities to do what you love in the world become blocked. It's like the needle gets stuck in the song track of, "I can't," "I don't know what to do" and "Something's wrong with me."

How can the fire of creativity burn when there is only stifling oppression? And how do you tap into the energy of creativity when you're locked in an invisible cage?

DESTRUCTION PREVAILS OVER CREATION

Instead of creating your life, you actually *unconsciously choose* the energy of destruction. In subtle yet pervasive ways, you destroy everything you desire to create. This may look like destroying or ending relationships, bankrupting yourself or indebting yourself financially, and/or being destructive with your body – and never realizing there's something else possible. It looks and feels like you're paddling upstream, always confronting a struggle, obstacle or catastrophe.

Why is this?

Because disharmony and conflict are familiar.

And harmony and peace are foreign.

The invisible cage is rooted in the lie that something's wrong with you. It's based in the story that you're limited and that you lack something. These judgements that you make of yourself (and potentially others, too) are focused on destroying you and keeping you small. They're not geared to creating a life of radical aliveness.

It sounds insane, I know. Why would anyone choose to destroy their life rather than create their life?

All you have to do, though, is look closely and be willing to be completely honest. Ask yourself:

Have I been creating or destroying my life?

Have I been creating or destroying my relationship?

Have I been creating or destroying my relationship with myself?

Have I been creating or destroying my relationship with money?

Have I been creating or destroying my relationship with my body?

GET HONEST WITH YOURSELF

As I described in the "Introduction," the first two decades of my life were filled with abuse: physical, sexual, emotional, mental, financial. It came from many places: family members, friends of family, the Church, the modeling agency, and healers.

I was told over and over all throughout my childhood that I was evil and I believed this lie. It became the cage that I lived in.

Throughout my healing process, I was determined to use my own experience of abuse as the catalyst for the Beyond Abuse Revolution and, later, the Live Your ROAR movement. To achieve this, however, I first had to get honest with myself and see how I was actually destroying versus creating my life, relationships, career, finances, body, health and my whole being.

For example, I never desired to let anyone close to me because I was afraid they, too, would see my evilness and run away screaming. How could I create anything other than destruction if I was evil and nobody would ever love me?

I also learned the language of unkindness growing up, so that's what I used in relationship as an adult. I created conflict rather than communion which resulted in divorce and desperation.

In my 20s, I overrode my body's needs and engaged in destructive patterns: drugs, sex and overeating. I had money, yet felt guilty that I had it and others didn't, so I paid for everyone else in an effort to try and buy their love.

All of these behaviors kept me trapped in the invisible cage of abuse, repeating the same abusive patterns that were familiar to me from my childhood. All I knew was to destroy myself and everything else in my life.

THE BRIDGE BEYOND THE CAGE

The turning point came for me when that graduate school professor reached out and asked me if I was okay, and this conversation with her became the bridge to a new chapter in my life. She helped me see there was another way of living beyond repeating the patterns of abuse.

I committed myself to finding the way out of the cage that kept me trapped in destruction rather than truly living my life. I became a Doctor of Psychology and studied dozens of healing modalities. Working with therapists and healers, I simultaneously walked my own healing journey while helping clients at the same time, guiding them on their own healing journey beyond the invisible cage of abuse.

Today, over two decades later, I've worked with thousands of clients around the world, and am deeply humbled and grateful that those early years, entrenched in so much abuse, have become the catalyst for kicking abuse in the caboose.

I'm excited to share the keys I've discovered for unlocking the cage of abuse because beyond the cage, beyond the bridge, is a way of living that's rooted in the energy of possibility and creativity.

This way of living is what I call *Radically Alive.*

WELCOME TO RADICAL ALIVENESS

Imagine the following...

You wake up with a spring in your step, happy to be alive and ready to see what else is possible for the day. From start to finish, your day is full of choice based on your desires and that, from those desires, everything is possible and you are a generative and creative magnet.

People love to be around you. You change the energy of everything around you just by being you.

Your relationships are based in communion and harmony. They're fun, easeful, joyful and mutual. Your body is healthy and vibrantly alive. You are energized. You have a special glow about you.

Your business is booming and the collaborators you have laugh and join with you in whatever you are creating. Each day is a new possibility of receiving money, support and possibilities.

Life is a joyous adventure. Laughter and lightness infuse your body. You are amazed to feel such an alliance with yourself.

People ask you what you did to change you and you respond with, "I chose me and happiness and created what I knew was possible."

Inspiring, isn't it?

This is the life that's waiting for you to choose it.

Let me introduce you to the keys to unlock yourself from the cage of abuse, so you, too, can walk across the bridge and experience Radical

Aliveness.

THE 4 C's: CHOOSE, COMMIT, COLLABORATE & CREATE

The 4 C's are keys that will unlock you from the lie and limitations you once bought into, and the destructive cycle that perpetuated your earlier abuse.

1. Choose You

What does it mean to "choose you?"

Well, you know what it's like when you're in a relationship with someone and you do everything in support of them and not you? That's an example of you **not** choosing you. When you do for others at the expense of yourself, you're making them more important than you. This is what happens in abuse: your desires and needs become irrelevant.

When you choose you, your needs and desires become important. You become a priority. You begin creating your life.

When you choose you, you can still be generous and be there for other people, yet **not** at the expense of you. You include yourself in all your choices and relationships.

What might you create when you choose you?

2. Commit to You

When you commit to yourself you commit to never giving in, never giving up, and never letting anyone or anything stop you. It's you committing to you to choose you every moment, every day.

In other words: you don't quit.

Ever.

My tenacity to overcome the first two decades of my life and all the abuse I experienced came from this place of committing to me. Once I realized that I was living in a cage of abuse and that there was something I could choose beyond the cage, I vowed to never quit till I was out of the cage and on the other side of the bridge from it.

I also vowed to empower as many others as possible to unlock themselves from the cage of abuse by choosing themselves and committing to their own lives as well.

When you commit to yourself, you commit to *being all of you in all of your relationships.* You don't separate from yourself to try to please or accommodate others. The paradox is that, as you commit to you, you actually become more available to commit to others in harmonious, mutually satisfying ways.

What might you create when you commit to you?

3. Collaborate with the Universe

Like I shared earlier, when you're inside the cage of abuse you may feel like you're paddling upstream and always confronting a struggle, obstacle or catastrophe. It feels like the world is out to get you.

I believed that for a long time, too. I thought everyone was against me and that I had to do everything myself.

It's a *lie.*

Because, the truth is, the Universe is actually conspiring to bless you and rooting for your greatest joy and success. All you have to do is collaborate with it by opening yourself to receiving the contribution and support of all the different people and possibilities that *desire* to give to you.

And it's as simple as asking.

When you're willing to ask – and receive – you'll discover that there's so much more available to you in creating your life.

What might you create when you collaborate with the Universe?

4. Create Your Life

You can initiate a new conversation with the Universe by asking the following questions:

➤ *What is fun for you?*
➤ *What lights you up?*
➤ *How might your life be different if you created your life for you?*
➤ *What would you choose for you when you're not focused on making other people your biggest priority?*

When you keep tapping into what you desire and allow that to be your biggest priority, you'll create an inspiring and expansive life for yourself.

You will be the creator, rather than the destroyer of your life.

And truly, how does it get any better than that®?

THE ENERGY OF CREATIVITY

The 4 C's will get you out of the cage and across the bridge into radical aliveness, one step at a time, one choice at a time so that, rather than destroying your life, you are now creating your life.

Begin first by choosing to question the cage – to see that it's made up of lies and limitations that are not true for you. You must be willing to let go of the old patterns of "I can't," "I don't know what to do," and "Something's wrong with me."

As you question the cage and ask what else is possible, you begin walking out of the cage and across the bridge to another possibility. The desire for something beyond the cage of abuse is the fuel that will carry you forward.

What is asking to be created now? Choose it! Be the space of possibility.

In the next chapter, you'll learn about a unique kind of energy you have available to you to create the life you choose.

Three

CREATING YOUR LIFE "FALLING TOGETHER"

"...And I'd say the world is full of wonderful things you haven't seen yet. Don't ever give up on the chance of seeing them."
~ JK Rowling (Twitter post)

As a healing practitioner, I play in the realm of consciousness to help people transform their lives and live radically alive. Because many of my clients come from some kind of abuse in their background, this transformation can be quite spectacular and dramatic.

If there's a "secret" to their success in making this leap, I'd say it was in discovering and owning their ability to step squarely into the energy of *I'm having it! No matter what.*

When you choose this space, you'll perceive a palpable expansion and density at the same time, like a ball of energy living inside a giant pinball machine, hurtling through space, bouncing off what's not working until, eventually, you land where you intended and chose.

This energy of *I'm having it!* engenders the idea that – no matter where you've come from, no matter what your story is, no matter what abuse, trauma or horrific tragedy has befallen you or your family, what relationships haven't worked out, the money you don't have or that you lost, or whatever conflicts you're embroiled in – you will not stop until you have what you desire.

So even though you're metaphorically in that pinball machine pinging from one side to another, two lengths forward and one back, you keep "cannon-balling" yourself into life with the awareness that – no matter what it is that you can't seem to get beyond – it's not working for you and you will not stop until that changes.

I'm having it! No matter what.

At first this can seem a little hard. It makes me think of the adage, "Work hard, play hard," and while it isn't that per se – because the *I'm having it!* energy is actually easy – it does take that tenacity of consciousness to keep charging forward, regardless of perceived blockages that seemingly reject you or are trying to stop you. In effect you say, "Okay, that didn't work. Choice creates awareness. *I'm having it! No matter what.* So what's the next step?"

And then go for it.

HOW FAR CAN YOU GO?

One of my clients, for example, heard the whispers of consciousness to have a baby at the same time her 10-year marriage was falling apart. She'd always wanted to have a baby, but for many reasons, it didn't work out. In spite of all this, it still gnawed at her.

During this period, she worked with me extensively to choose to listen to the whisper and, as she did, everything started changing rapidly. She was determined to have a child on her own no matter what and began making the big decisions required to create her desired life, which included choosing to get a divorce and have a baby on her own.

At first she hit roadblock after roadblock. Fertility doctors wanted nothing to do with it because going through a divorce muddled the picture. Then, once she did get pregnant, she faced discrimination as a single mother at her company, even though she was a high-ranking employee in a prestigious position.

But the more her life fell apart, the more she stayed committed to the process and worked to clear her consciousness.

In essence, she said, "I'm having this child. I feel the energy of this spirit around me and I'm not going to give that up. I choose to create this. What do I need to do to make that occur and what will work for me?" And in this, she listened to the whispers of consciousness about the spirit of this baby and found a way to get pregnant, and took on the pragmatics of that. She chose to utilize the tools of energy healing and the *I'm having it!* energy of 'I choose me no matter what.'"

COMMAND AND DEMAND

No matter what isn't working, somehow, some way, there will be an opening, even if it feels as tiny as a pinhole that you have to squeeze yourself to get through. This doesn't, however, require you to bend, fold, mutilate, or squeeze yourself out of you to do it.

Instead, you're "squeezing" yourself out of the obligations, oaths, vows, contracts, genetics, ancestry, belief systems, and physical reality that tells you, "You can't have it all. You can't say what you really desire. You can't create your life in the way that you really desire it."

When you do cross the line into this energy, it may intimidate some of the people around you. They may mistake making a demand for yourself with "being demanding," particularly if they grew up with abusive or "demanding" parents or others and don't understand the distinction. Making a demand is a powerful stance of "I'm having this!" whereas the other can have an abusive edge to it. They couldn't be more fundamentally different.

Unfortunately, when it comes down to it, most people don't actually believe they can command and demand their life, to create it with the ease that truly can be, and so they live their lives as "a waiting game." They wait for someone else's willingness to change, someone else's creation and success for them to jump in on and be something.

Riding along on another's coat tails like this, they become more of a parasitic sucking energy than a generative, creating energy for themselves, for their business, and for their relationships. It's the opposite of *I'm having it!* This is more like, "They're having it and I'm going to see what I can get from it!"

It's like saying, "Oh, somebody else has got something and is doing something? Let me just join with them and do the most minimal amount I can, show up as little as I can but demand to be compensated" – as if they run the business – "and be a part of something bigger than me but never be the demand for me with me and with others."

Of course, this does nothing to further and transform their life or be the change agent in collaboration with others or the earth.

This complacency people live in puts them in a state of ennui, perpetually in limbo, waiting for "what is" to change. Of course, they desire something more and talk about it all the time, but they never get around to generating and creating. Their thoughts tend to circle back on themselves like a tiger chasing its tail:

"Why does this keep happening to me? Everything's such a struggle. Nothing ever works for me no matter how hard I try. Why is everything so hard? How come it works for others but not for me?"

Their lives are confined to a very small area, which I've described earlier, as a kind of self-imposed cage with energetic "bars" which keeps them imprisoned.

Freeing Yourself

The cage of abuse is made up of four "pillars" which I call the "4 D's." Later, in Chapter Six, we'll explore them more fully, but for now it's helpful to know what they are:

- ➤ Denying
- ➤ Defending
- ➤ Disconnecting
- ➤ Dissociating

In my work, I help people identify this invisible cage so they can not only unlock it and walk out into freedom, but cross over the "bridge" into Radical Aliveness into *I'm having it! No matter what* energy.

If you'll recall from the previous chapter, Radical Aliveness also has four components – the "4 C's":

- ➤ Choosing for you
- ➤ Committing to you
- ➤ Collaborating and knowing that the universe is conspiring to bless you
- ➤ Creating the life you desire

When you're waiting you're not choosing. You're leaving your back door open so nothing gets created other than the trauma and drama of the pinball machine. This is destruction and disempowerment and what keeps you locked in the invisible cage of abuse.

IT'S ALL ABOUT BIG ENERGY

I'm having it! is all about big energy – or pronoia.

In his book, *Pronoia Is the Antidote for Paranoia, Revised and Expanded: How the Whole World Is Conspiring to Shower You with Blessings*, Rob Brezsny describes it as "the antidote for paranoia. [Pronoia] is the understanding that the universe is fundamentally friendly. It's a mode of training your senses and intellect so you're able to perceive the fact that life always gives you exactly what you desire, exactly when you demand it."

You can choose to become an intensity of which nothing can stop you, no matter what. Yes, you might spin for a little while, or bounce back and forth in that pinball machine until you become the pinball wizard – focused, direct, demanding and deliciously choosing what you are desiring. And more often than not, everything may begin to fall apart and away at first (and you will likely fight that at first), but I implore you to receive it as a sign that things are working, that the universe is conspiring to bless you. This falling apart and away is a natural and essential part of the creating process.

A PERSONAL EXAMPLE

Recently I was getting ready for a six-week tour I'd been planning when suddenly, out of the blue, unexpected financial demands flooded me. My immediate reaction was, "Oh, I can't leave now and do all this. I need to work more and pay all this – that's the pragmatic thing to do. I shouldn't be getting on a plane now to go somewhere to take care of myself or facilitate others. How can I go there when I don't have everything nailed down?"

Clearly, this was the voice of "I'm not having it," the one that says,

"See? I told you...you can't have it." Funny how whenever we are moving forward we actually enact the trauma of things coming toward us to block us from being the wizard, the magical creator we truly be.

As if that weren't enough, at the same time things fell apart on the romantic front when my "enjoyable other" left our relationship and ended 'us' unilaterally. I would have probably chosen differently and said, "Hey, what can we do together?" totally aware that sometimes you can't do it together – you have to do it yourself.

So what can you do when someone makes a choice and it's not your choice? You choose, too. That's an *I'm having it! No matter what* choice.

So, I chose to go away for those six weeks, I chose to let go completely of that relationship, I chose me and I chose to know that the universe will conspire to bless me and that all on the financial front will generate new possibilities easily and effortlessly.

And here's the amazing knowing that comes along with listening to those whispers and choosing you along with the blessings of the universe: All worked out better than I could have ever imagined. Yes, there have been bumps in the road and yet nothing less than expansiveness has joined me on this journey. I am forever changed and committed to me.

I'm Having It! I Choose It! I Choose Me!

In this energy is a willingness to let it all go. You have to be willing to lose everything to have everything. And, while this may seem like a bad thing, if you look closely, you'll usually discover that most of it is stuff you didn't want anyway because, on some level, it wasn't fully supporting you.

Let's face it...

If you want something that's a "10," you'll probably have to let go of the "9" you've been holding onto, although initially letting go of the form and structure of that may be the hardest part. In my own case, I didn't have a problem letting go or having any of what I shared above change. The difficulty I got stuck in was "believing" it had to look a certain way to fit into this reality – until I got with the spirit of the change and made choices to keep choosing me and to keep the demand radically alive of *I'm having it! No matter what.* No matter who I lose, what I lose, who leaves my life, whose life I leave, I will never give up on me.

If you're paying attention when life is falling apart like this, you can actually feel and perceive the energy of change – often it's the real change you've been demanding for some time. That's how it felt to me as I watched my entire life come apart at the seams right in front of my eyes, melting into liquid and feeding the earth. But even with all the stickiness and gooiness and squeezing with emotions, I knew there wasn't anything occurring in the *I'm having it!* energy I wouldn't have had change.

In these situations, I've found that the best thing to do is somewhat counter-intuitive – just play with it, play with the energy and ride the pinball machine through the pinhole to everything expansive and light. We often give up right before the magic arrives.

Because, here's the deal...

What if everything is actually falling together?

I'm having it! energy may look like everything's falling apart, yet what if it's all really falling together?

Certainly, this is the moment where you could make that pragmatic choice, and give up on what you really demand and desire. Or, you could say, "No, I can create this, I can do this, I require this, I'm collaborating with the universe, I'm choosing myself and I'm committing to myself and creating my life falling together."

You have to know that the universe does conspire to bless you, as you be the demand for you, even when the appearance of things is changing. If you look out into nature, you'll see this is the natural order of things. What happens after a fire in the woods? New life breathes and grows.

In creativity, there's always a breakdown, a movement into an expansive space of choice and creation. Similar to the Chinese practice of Feng Shui, where you consciously move things out and around and rearrange to create a more harmonious and prospering environment, the *I'm having it!* energy is the movement of the molecules within you to embody the demand of living radically alive beyond anything you've allowed thus far.

IT'S ALL A CHOICE - *Your* CHOICE

Being the generative force, the *I'm having it!* energy, is the opposite of waiting. It's an excuse, really, waiting for things to "unfold," waiting for that "sign," or for whatever you're waiting for to be obvious. You put yourself in a position of possibly waiting a very long time.

I ask people, "Haven't you waited long enough for someone else to be the demand in your life? What if you are the energy you're waiting for?"

Do you realize you can be a demand for you even when joining with another? That's what I've created with my team at Live Your ROAR LLC headquarters. Everyone has become the catalyst to moving beyond abuse and living radically alive. No one rides on my coattails. We all ask the business what it desires and what it would like to have and then we go about creating that. We live as the demand and the universe blesses us with our requests.

If you're someone who has the energy of *I'm having it! No matter what*, then being around people who are "waiting" may prove to be challenging, to say the least. For example, let's say you're a small business owner and have an employee who has issues around receiving money. Obviously, you probably weren't aware of this when you hired them and put them in a position where they're accountable for money.

Later, whenever you ask them about the status of a payment, you notice they make excuses or say things like, "Yes, I talked to the customer and they said they paid," even though your bank has informed you that payment was declined. You keep going back and forth, and this happens again and again.

What's happening is that, because they refuse to receive money for themselves, they unconsciously block receiving money on behalf of the business, as well. In effect, this creates a waiting game for receiving money and can destroy businesses and relationships.

When it comes to money, receiving and collecting it demands a personal power to choose what you desire beyond what you have. In other words, it demands the *I'm having it! No matter what* energy.

Being the generative energy of *I'm having it!* is a no holds barred, go forward and create it space. Regardless of where you are or where you want to be, the creative process is always the same and you can pretty well assume that, when it gets close enough to taste it, things will start to heat up, implode, or fall apart.

It's at this precise moment you have to let go and step fully into *I'm having it!* so it can all fall together in alignment with the universe and with your choice. This makes it all about you and your willingness to allow the bigness of this reality that is here to collaborate with you and bless you.

However... there is a 'catch.'

Your willingness to allow all this support on your behalf presupposes an ability to actually receive, and I have found that this is where people who have been abused often run into problems.

Frankly, they don't do it all that well.

So let's move on and find out what it takes to become a 'wide receiver.'

Four

Kindness...The Great Wide River Flowing in You

Constant kindness can accomplish much. As the sun makes ice melt,
kindness causes misunderstanding, mistrust, and hostility to evaporate.
Albert Schweitzer

You were born to be kind – and I'm not just making this up.

According to an interview in *Scientific American* called, "Forget Survival of the Fittest: It is Kindness that Counts," kindness is 'hard-wired' into our brain.

Not that everybody defaults to it, but it's there as an innate gift.

My intention in this chapter is to shine the light on it in a way you might not have thought of it before because, truly, kindness is much more than simply a good idea, or something you do to be 'nice.'

It's actually a force, or power, that, as Albert Schweitzer so elegantly phrased it, 'causes misunderstanding, mistrust, and hostility to evaporate.'

And if you have had any form of abuse in your life – past or present – you're going to want to know about this inner friend.

Personally, I didn't make friends with it until I was in my 20s –

after my Family Violence professor showed me what kindness was by approaching me and asking if I was okay. She'd noticed my body language, which had formed around two decades of abuse, trauma and judgement I'd lived with growing up. My shoulders were hunched up and over, nearly to my ears, in an effort to protect myself from beatings handed to me physically, verbally, and energetically.

I had other obvious kinds of behaviors, too, that came from the sexual abuse I'd endured as a child model. At least, they were obvious to the trained eye. These patterns of abuse had become internalized on many levels – both in the way I walked and held myself and in the way I communicated to myself and others.

Today, I refer to this as the 'somatics of trauma,' those ways of being that become a solidified part of our physical and energetic structure, integrated and locked in to our cellular and molecular structure.

Sounds heavy, doesn't it? Like an impregnable fortress.

Well, the good news is that, if it is, then kindness is like the siege engine that will break it down.

THE FORTRESS OF JUDGEMENT

Here's the thing about judgement...

It's been around a very long, long time – thousands and thousands of years. Humans have perfected it as a 'skill.' But that's not the worst of it.

Judgement is woven into the fabric of our DNA. We inherit it when we're born into the collective consciousness, generational lines of it that get carried down through time and passed to us. That is, until someone breaks the cycle. It's that 'sins of the father' thing.

So what does it take to break the cycle?

Excellent question...

But before we do that, let's look at what judgement perpetuates in your life *if you don't.*

> Judgement keeps you lying to you and locks you back into an 'invisible cage of abuse,' which keeps you locked away from you, from others, from living and certainly from creating the life you desire.

> Judgement is a form of constriction and limitation, a self-destructive device and a pervasive form of *self-abuse.* It's the opposite of expansion that keeps you small and struggling, victim-like and powerless, armored and numb. As a result, you stop generating and creating beyond the cage; instead, you perpetrate you and keep the abuse cycle going.

> When you judge yourself, you become your own eternal jailer and further lock yourself into the wrongness of you. Judgement returns you to the comfort of what you know (how "bad" you are) and guarantees that you never have to be more than you are right now. It solidifies the invisible cage of abuse.

> When you judge another, you're actually defending, disconnecting, denying and dissociating from what you're not willing to see about yourself. I call these the '4 D's.' By design, it isolates and separates you, the opposite of oneness and belonging.

> Judgement is actually something I call 'forced receiving' because, in essence, you're forcing yourself to accept

someone else's judgements, particularly where you have been abused and had to receive something you didn't want – that you were forced to receive. As a result, you develop sharp, arrow-like 'quills,' like a porcupine, that can and will repel people from getting too close.

Judgements are resistances to reality that we use to protect ourselves. Many of them we learned as children either because we saw them or heard them, or because we decided them in reaction to something happening to us. These decisions then became habits of thought, the lens we see through and live by on autopilot for the rest of the flight.

The problem is that, by continuing to use them in our daily encounters with life, we cut off any other possibility we might otherwise be, do or have.

And it's to this end – clearing and transforming these judgements in order to live a freely joyful life – that I have spent the majority of my career and healing practice.

In fact, I have a name for it.

I call it living your ROAR – a Radically, Orgasmically, Alive Reality.

How does it get any better than that?

You're All Possibility

Your true nature is unbounded creativity, abundance, and expansion.

When you're sitting behind a desk in a cubbyhole it may not feel that way, so the best way I know to really appreciate and grow in your awareness of this knowledge is by hanging out in nature more often.

You don't even have to do anything...

It will come to you intuitively.

One of the reasons being in nature is so powerful is that the earth is the one place where judgement can't reside. It's the place you can return to again and again to release your judgements and feel the peace and possibilities of expansion. It's actually a kindness to gift your judgements to the earth.

By gifting the manure of your judgements to the earth, you literally fertilize a new possibility for yourself and everyone else.

So what is possible?

For one thing, once you let yourself out of the cage of abuse that keeps you in a 'victim' story, the whole world's wide open to you. Out there in the wild open space, you realize you have other choices for how to live and relate to yourself and others.

For example, in my case, when I discovered who I actually was beyond a shutdown, miserable, self-destructive girl, I learned I was kind, brilliant, phenomenal and funny.

Who and what is waiting to be seen by you?

As you exercise new choices, you begin to grow more confident. The old patterns of abuse no longer have power over you. You now have the power over your abuse and, with that, the power to choose a new life for yourself.

You no longer create your life from destruction, but from choice.

I know that may seem like a tall order because, quite frankly, you may be more committed to the victim story than the possibility of life beyond it. I see this time and time again in people when they first come to see me. You may feel like a victim of circumstance, as I did for so long, like there's nothing you can do to change it.

But it's a lie...

Plain and simple.

KINDNESS AS A GENERATIVE ENERGY

It's common for children who've been abused to believe they're bad and wrong, but it took that conversation with my Family Violence professor in undergraduate school, and her help, to realize I wasn't worthless.

This professor was the first person who ever asked me if I was okay, and this single act of kindness flooded me with the awareness of how *not* okay I was. With her support, I began to see there was something I could do to overcome my past abuse – that I could go beyond surviving, even beyond thriving, one day.

It was as though she'd passed me the secret key to unlock myself from the cage of my own abuse.

I began to see the abusive, destructive patterns I was perpetuating through reckless behavior and I committed to choosing differently. I didn't do this on my own. It was through professional support and confidential conversations that I was finally able to release the victim story I had been living for nearly three decades.

When I let go of that, the invisible cage began to crumble away, too. I no longer needed the barriers and walls I'd erected to protect myself as I slowly realized I had other choices for how I lived and how I related to myself and others.

And it all began with that single act of kindness which, indeed, caused 'misunderstanding, mistrust, and hostility to evaporate.'

Obviously, not every moment of kindness is going to do this. Kindness wears many faces. It ranges from the simplest act – like a smile – that takes no more than a second, to extravagant offerings of help. It can be random and come out of the blue or given in response to someone's needs.

In truth, it's probably more natural to you than any other approach because, as I said in the beginning, kindness is *already in you*.

You don't have to go far to find it, although when you're locked up in judgement it can seem impossible to access. So, if you're having a hard time being kind, begin looking around for the underlying judgements blocking the view.

One way to do this is asking questions like these:

➤ *"Am I being judgement or kindness with this?" – whether it's in relationship to money, relationship, your body, or something else.*
➤ *"Does this feel expansive or restrictive?"*
➤ *"Does this feel light or heavy?"*

By committing to you and accepting kindness for yourself – from yourself and others – a new space of energy and consciousness can show up – a place of receiving that is at once vibrant, alive, potent, juicy and all *deliciously you.*

Kindness ushers in a peak vitality that only requires four things, which I call the '4 E's':

1. *Embracing* what's true for you
2. *Examining* what you are actually looking at
3. *Expanding* into a new possibility, awareness, and kindness
4. *Embodying* the change and the truth of you

In a very real way, learning kindness is like learning a new language. In my own case, it was not a language I was familiar with. It wasn't my 'first' language, the one I heard and spoke at home. And it took practicing over time to not only learn it, but to then become fluent in it.

And, like language, it is a creative, generative energy – exactly what it takes to create a new life filled with the energy of expansion.

The beautiful thing is that, by giving up judgements and harnessing the power of kindness and gentleness, you can dissolve all the uncaring ways that you've experienced and let go of the need to protect yourself.

You can finally shed the quills and be open to receiving bountiful life – to truly be the gift you are for yourself and the world. In this place of no barriers, you will discover a softer, more vulnerable space... at once sacred and safe.

It is here that the energy of receiving flows free and easy like a great river.

You only need choose it, step into it and let it move you along its wide and generous path. It's all yours simply for the choosing.

In the next chapter, we're going to talk more about receiving and, specifically, 'seduced receiving.'

Five

Seduced Receiving to Be the Gift You Truly Be

From then on, I realized this is what I want to do, what I'm supposed to do: Giving energy and receiving it back through applause. I love it. That's my world. I love it. I enjoy it. I live for it.
~ Erykah Badu

Hopefully, by now, you're beginning to sense that you are here to live a life far greater than you've imagined thus far.

No matter what.

Perhaps your "what" – like mine – is overcoming decades of abuse and living radically alive. If I could go on to create a life beyond my wildest dreams, I know you can do this, too. In fact, I know this for all my clients.

Whether or not you struggled with abuse, chances are, if you're reading this book, there is something in your life that feels like a trap, a cage, some way you feel locked out of the possibility of receiving.

The good news is the key to unlock the prison of *not receiving you* rests inside of you.

What is Receiving?

Receiving is an action you take with no barriers to anyone or anything. It's a space of vulnerability, of openness, and of oneness with everything. Receiving has no boundaries or obligations. It's not forced or demanded, it's simply a way of being the space of *you* in the energy of *you* as the consciousness of *you!*

To be the energy, space and consciousness of you, you only need imagine that you are as big as the universe and the earth. In that bigness, you are everything and nothing at the same time. You're a part of it all because there's literally a molecular communion that exists which includes awareness with and for and about everything.

This energy I call 'receiving' gives you total power, total choice, total awareness, total strength from the vulnerability contained within the willingness to be the biggest you there is.

What would the world be like if we all lived as this space of energy?

Unfortunately, the energy of receiving on this planet has been mired with wars, conflict, abuse and terror, which is *not* the energy of receiving at all. Receiving creates; abuse destroys. Receiving generates; wars destroy. Receiving produces communion; conflicts form separations. Receiving builds sustainability; terror extinguishes choice. To choose is to receive.

To receive is to choose beyond the form and structure of this reality.

Receiving, then, is the greatest weapon we all have to abolish outdated modes of being – simply by being the energy of total allowance.

What is the Energy of Receiving?

Receiving is the energy that's required to live the life you desire. It's also the energy you may be blocking if you experienced any form of abuse.

How do you know if you're blocking the energy of receiving?

> ➤ You crave communion, but feel stuck in less-than-satisfying relationships.
> ➤ You desire success in your career, but have hit a plateau and don't understand why you aren't earning more.
> ➤ You dream of being vibrantly healthy, but struggle with some chronic condition.

In my own healing process, I've discovered there's a direct connection between abuse and the tendency to block receiving. Yet, there are ways to unblock the energy of receiving in your life. Below I've listed five steps that can help you:

5 Steps to Unblock the Energy of Receiving

Step 1: Acknowledge the Invisible Porcupine
How often do you get prickly when someone comes towards you?

I call it being the "invisible porcupine." It's a phenomenon I know very well, both in myself and in the clients I've worked with over the past two decades.

You know where these quills come from? Your past abuse. Once upon a time the world wasn't safe for you so you created these quills as your best attempt to protect yourself. The quills worked well back then; they're just outdated now.

How much are you uninviting into your life with these quills?

Just like you hoped the quills would keep your abuser away, they now keep love, money, clients and all else at a "safe" distance. A safe distance blocks receiving because you're always looking out for when the catastrophe will occur.

Is it time to update your hard drive?

The first step to unblocking yourself from the energy of receiving is to acknowledge that you've been an invisible porcupine with quills armed and ready to defend 24/7 by embodying a self-defense posturing for attack all the time.

Step 2: Weed Out Stories That Block Receiving

When you experienced abuse you were forced to "receive" something you didn't wish to receive. In that moment you created a story that it's not safe to receive in any form. Love? Money? Health? All becomes dangerous.

For me, receiving meant receiving judgement. It meant doing what my mom said so I wouldn't be beaten. It meant being and living other people's realities with a desperate desire to get nurturance and love (which I never got, except in the form of money and objects and ultimately abuse).

What does receiving mean to you?

What stories have you told yourself about receiving that keep the quills in place? Are you willing to let those stories go?

Who or what have you misidentified and misapplied as receiving that is actually defending?

Step 3: Recognize the Quills Hurt Both Ways

Just like the "quills" of the invisible porcupine point outwards and keep everything in life (love, money, health, etc.) at a "safe" distance, they also point inward and keep you from coming forward into your own life.

At some point, perhaps a long time ago, you learned it wasn't "safe" to come forward. In your attempt to escape your abuse, or tell someone about your abuse, you may have disconnected or dissociated. Either way, you went away from yourself to try to keep yourself safe.

So you keep poking yourself with your own quills in the form of judgements and stories that it's not safe to be seen or heard.

Do you know what the most painful thing about all of this? You're living your own life at a "safe" distance from yourself and never fully receiving the beauty and potency of *you*.

You never get to *receive* you.

And frankly, you probably have little to no knowledge of who you are – who you truly be – because you've always been the quills and never allowed the real you to emerge.

This is the real epidemic of abuse given this reality: Us divorcing from ourselves.

Just like Steps 1 and 2, you need to acknowledge the quills hurt you, too, and let go of the stories you've made about what it means to come forward in your own life, and the way to do this this is through forgiveness and acceptance. These are the keys to this step and they're not for anyone but you.

To forgive and accept yourself is the greatness kindness you can receive for you.

Step 4: Release Forced Receiving

As mentioned in Step 2, when you experienced abuse you were forced to "receive" something you didn't wish to receive. This is called "forced receiving."

How does this past experience impact how you give to others today?

Have you gotten away from forced receiving or are you actually repeating the cycle? Forced receiving sets you up to be rejected again and again. It's what keeps you from true communion in every aspect of your life.

How do you know if you're trapped in the cycle of "forced receiving"?

You think you know what's best for others: "Here, eat this." "Do this." "Take this.") You give what you think others "should" have instead of what they ask for.

Essentially, you're living as superior to everyone and unaware about everything. Just because you can do things for others doesn't actually mean they want it. Forcing someone to receive what you think is best for them suggests you know better and are smarter and are more aware, which completely devalues them. It's a total disrespect of their being.

So stop forcing your will on others, and allow them to be who they be and receive them for all of it with no point of view. Simple curiosity about another goes a long way in creating relationships from receiving and allowing.

So how do you move beyond "forced receiving" and into another possibility?

Step 5: Embrace Seduced Receiving

It all starts with awareness. Once you see how you're using "forced receiving" you can choose something else.

Why not try *seduced receiving?*

Granted, seduction may sound a little dangerous to you, particularly if you experienced abuse as a result of being or doing something that "seduced" another to force themselves upon you.

So just a reminder, like in Step 2, here you can choose to weed out this story that blocks you from receiving.

What if there's a "safe" way to be seductive?

And what if "seduced receiving" is essential to invite into your life all that you desire? our perpetrators attempted to take something they had no right to. Keeping seduction or orgasmic living away from you keeps the perpetrators in charge of you. Becoming the art of your own seduction restores a space of embodiment that has always been within you even before the abuse. Claim it, it's yours.

With seduced receiving, you're being the invitation for what you desire. You become the energy of the possibility of greater health, relationship, money, and business.

What would it take for your kindness and gentleness to be so strong that it dissolved all the uncaring ways that you've experienced (and that you continue to try to "protect" yourself against with your quills)?

It's in this place of seduced receiving that you truly be the gift you be: for yourself and the world.

In this place of soft vulnerability, you let go of the quills; there are no more barriers. Here, the energy of receiving is flowing free and easy.

The space, energy and consciousness of receiving is vibrant, alive, potent, juicy and just plain yummy.

It's yummy because it's you being you.

It's alive because you're embodying your energy.

It's potent because your greatest strength is kindness.

It's vibrant and juicy because you're allowing all of you to be gifted in and with this reality, which changes everyone and everything in and around you at the molecular level.

Seduced receiving is the greatest form of vitality on this planet. We all have it intrinsically and, the more you embrace it, the more you will connect with the energy of expansion, as you'll discover in the next chapter.

Six

THE ENERGY OF EXPANSION

The personal life deeply lived always expands into truths beyond itself
~ Anais Nin

When I was only seven years old, I remember looking out my bedroom window at the moon with a prayer heavy on my heart. By then, I had already experienced all kinds of physical, sexual, emotional and mental abuse that continued well into my 20's. And it was at that young age I committed my life to getting myself out of what I call the invisible cage of abuse because I knew something else was possible.

I vowed that one day I would find a way beyond the life that I was living. I vowed that I would do what it took to create a world where all children could lay their head on their pillows at night and rest peacefully.

It took years, a lot of support and a lot of courage to practice the art of the energy of expansion. I've found a way to thrive beyond childhood sexual abuse and have supported many people in living beyond their own abuse to create limitless lives.

I travel the world facilitating classes. I have a radio show on *Voice*

America where I reach thousands of listeners every week with my show, "Beyond Abuse, Beyond Therapy, Beyond Anything."

You could say I kept my promise to that little 7-year-old me.

I chose to never give up, never give in and always go for what else was infinitely possible. And, currently, I'm committed to eradicating and eliminating abuse off this planet so that more children and more adults live the empowered, expansive existence that is their birthright.

It's Not *ALL* About Abuse

To be clear, you don't have to have experienced abuse as a child to find yourself locked in your own invisible cage, one that keeps you from being the energy of expansion and the greatness you desire.

The invisible cage knows no one genre and is more than happy to ensnare anyone.

If you've been caught in its grips, you're probably ready to break free and create the world you know is possible. Perhaps, like me, you made a vow to do this for yourself, but you're just not sure how to do this.

I invite you to explore the ways the "invisible cage" has kept you from your greatness so that you, too, can move beyond the constriction of the cage and into an embodiment of the energy of expansion.

Recognizing the Energy of Expansion

If you're going on this journey, it helps to know what you're seeking to create. The energy of expansion is:

> ➤ Knowing your greatness and the magical being you truly be

- ➤ Living a life of fun, freedom, joy and radical aliveness
- ➤ Recognizing there are infinite possibilities always
- ➤ Asking for and receiving that which you desire
- ➤ Experiencing communion with yourself and others
- ➤ Gifting that which is uniquely yours to the world
- ➤ Choosing to create an empowered life beyond any limits

Pretty fantastic, wouldn't you agree? Imagine what kind of life you can create when you embody this energy of expansion.

In order to fully embrace and operate from this powerful energy, let's look at three of the biggest limitations of the invisible cage and how to move beyond them to embody the energy of expansion you truly be.

From Victimization to Empowerment

As a child I became pretty shut down. Nothing I did made a difference: I still got abused. I grew up believing there was nothing I could do to escape abuse. I was a victim to it.

And I carried this victim story into my 20's – I drank, partied, did drugs and engaged in other reckless behavior to try and escape the pain of my past abuse. I didn't care about myself. I didn't know then how common it is for children who've been abused to believe they're bad and wrong.

The journey beyond the victim story led me through the invisible cage to me and ultimately out of the cage to who I truly am. I discovered who I actually was beyond the shutdown miserable self-destructive girl. I learned I was kind, brilliant, phenomenal and funny.

I also realized I had other choices for how I lived and how I related to myself and others. As I exercised new choices I grew more confident.

The old patterns I faced directly and acknowledged their destruction of me. I then chose to create my living from what's light and right for me. I chose to give myself the possibility of creating something so completely different and yet so connected to who I always was despite the abuse.

What about you?

Is the "victim story" ruling your life? Have you been repeating the abuse cycle through self-destructive patterns too, and can you see how disempowering this is?

What if you can actually create your life from choice rather than destruction?

If you experienced any form of abuse in your life, or any kind of "wrongness," you may be more committed to the poor me story rather than the possibility of life beyond it. You may feel like a victim to circumstance, as I did for so long, like there's nothing you can do to change it. Every time I ever said there was nothing I could do to change my life, I knew I was lying. The choice I made became the difference between me and my feelings. I realized I am not my feelings and that I am my choices.

But, if you choose it, you can let this be a "phase" in your journey from the invisible cage to the energy of expansion. Are you ready to let go of the no choice story? If so, the following steps can help guide you.

3 Steps to Move Beyond Victimization and into Empowerment

1. Get support from a professional

Often times the same people you share your issues with are the people – family or friends – who helped create those issues. Talking with a professional accelerates your own movement in the journey out of victimization. Sharing what you would like to create with another and collaborating together from empowerment with and for your choices speaks volumes in moving you beyond your abuse. It's a fail safe plan to living radically alive. The healing professionals I worked with have become my allies in healing. I now allow myself to be that for others as I am that for myself. Never judge how long or what path the road takes, just keep choosing beyond the constriction of what was never yours in the first place.

2. Share your story and release all your secrets

Secrets keep you in the role of victim. They create shame and keep you disempowered and stuck in constriction and limitation. For every secret, you have to hold in about 25 reasons and justifications to keep that secret in place. Those secrets become dead weight and disillusion you from the authenticity you desire. And oddly enough those secrets are not even yours. They usually are the perpetrators or judgments of others put on you to keep you from being you. Judgment is a real epidemic in this reality especially around abuse.

3. Choose to let go of – and move beyond - the "victim story"

When you let go of your story and move beyond it, you begin to step into being the magic you truly be. You discover the energy of expansion available to you beyond the cage. There is an art to letting go of your story and that is to make a choice to create what you actually like to be and do. The abuse 'feels' like you never had choice. In that moment, you did not, in the years after you do every second of every day. I decided to have my story be what I create now and not what I created based on what occurred years ago.

As you move beyond the old story of you, you'll begin to experience the energy of expansion: freedom, joy and your own greatness. You'll begin to see more possibilities for yourself and your life, and you'll discover new sources of your own potency in surprising places. This will awaken in you the acknowledgment that you have always been you beyond the abuse and before the abuse. The abuse never has to define you as you are so much more and always are.

From Armoring to Vulnerability

When my mom swore at me and called me names, I didn't cry or let on how upset I was. I just did what was asked, got it over with, and went to my room to hide. When she beat me, I 'steeled up' and braced myself. I knew not to cry because she would only hit me harder. If I just took it and put on my invisible "armor" by not crying, I knew it would be over sooner.

I grew up believing that I was safer if I was tough. I developed really thick armor to protect my soft insides. This way my abusers only got my armor; they never fully "got" me.

As I talked about in an earlier chapter, I call this type of behavior 'armoring the invisible porcupine phenomenon.' It's so important to understand that I dedicated two entire radio shows to this topic (you can find the free recordings for these on my website at www.DrLisaCooney.com.) Just like a porcupine defends itself with sharp quills, you too might be wearing armor made of invisible quills. It's your best attempt to protect yourself from a world that doesn't seem safe.

But how expansive can you be when you're constantly defending yourself?

Just like you hoped the quills would keep an abuser away, they now keep relationships, money, clients and all else at a "safe" distance.

These quills block you from receiving the life you desire because it feels dangerous to receive anything.

How much are you uninviting into your life now with these quills?

And just like the quills of the invisible porcupine point outwards and keep everything in life (relationship, money, clients, etc.) at a "safe" distance, they also point inwards and keep you from coming forward into your own life.

At some point, perhaps a long time ago, you learned it wasn't "safe" to come forward. In your attempt to escape your abuse, or tell someone about your abuse, you may have disconnected or dissociated. Either way, you went away from yourself to try to keep yourself safe.

So you keep poking yourself with your own quills in the form of judgements and the story that it's not safe to be you. You keep yourself small, perhaps even invisible, to try and escape any perceived danger that may still be "out there."

Do you want to know the most painful thing about this?

You're living your own life at an "armored and safe" distance from yourself, never fully receiving the beauty and potency of *you*. Never experiencing the strength of your vulnerability.

Vulnerability is being *you* without the armor, without the defenses.

It took being in relationship with therapists, healers, partners and ultimately, myself, to trust that I could be "safe" if I removed my armor. Over time, I finally did release both my inner and outer quills.

And, as my quills dissolved, I discovered a new level of vulnerability that served me in a much greater capacity.

In this soft open space, I experienced communion with myself and others like I had never known before. I was able to ask for and receive what I truly desired. And I felt more alive than ever before because I was finally receiving myself and my life fully.

I discovered there is a potency in vulnerability that looks and feels a whole lot different from the strength of "steeling up." In fact, this potency is the best "protection" you could ever truly require.

A bit of warning, though...

When the armor is gone you may feel a little "naked" or overexposed – and this is completely normal. Nothing is wrong. It's just your soft inner space becoming more exposed to a life of communion with yourself beyond the armor.

Still, there's one final pervasive aspect of the invisible cage that will block you from the energy of expansion unless you learn how to move beyond it.

From Judgement to Kindness

Judgement is the opposite of expansion. It's a form of constriction and limitation, and a pervasive form of self-abuse.

When you judge another you're actually defending, disconnecting, denying and dissociating from what you're not willing to see about yourself. Judgement keeps you lying to you and locks you back into the invisible cage of abuse, which keeps you locked away from you, from others, from living and certainly from creating the life you desire.

When you judge yourself, you become your own eternal jailer and further lock yourself into the wrongness of you. Judgement returns you to the comfort of what you know (how "bad" you are) and guarantees that you never have to be more than you are right now. It solidifies the invisible cage of abuse.

Judgement keeps you small and struggling, victim-like and powerless, armored and numb. As a result, you stop generating and creating beyond the cage; instead, you perpetrate you and keep the abuse cycle going.

How is this a kindness to you? To anyone?

The only way to get beyond the cage and into the energy of expansion is to get beyond judgement, and there are six steps that can help you.

6 Steps to Access the Space of No Judgement

1. Sit in a quiet space, close your eyes, and take a few deep breaths
2. Expand your energy into the earth
3. Offer your judgements to the earth as a contribution
4. Open up to receive the contribution the earth can be for you
5. Bring your energy back into yourself without your judgements
6. Notice what you're aware of

The earth is the one place where judgement can't reside. It's the place you can return to again and again to release your judgements and feel the peace and possibilities of expansion. It's actually a kindness to gift your judgements to the earth. By gifting the manure of judgement to the earth, you fertilize a new possibility for yourself and everyone else.

In the space of no judgement is kindness. Kindness is the truth of who you be and what you've always been.

Kindness is a generative energy. I have discovered after traveling the world and working with thousands of people that kindness is what's required to move beyond judgement, beyond abuse and beyond limitation. This generative energy is what creates a new life filled with the energy of expansion.

As an exercise, take a moment to imagine...

➢ *What would occur in 50 years on this planet if you chose kindness?*

➢ *What would occur if you released the victim story and chose the path of empowerment?*

➢ *What would occur if you released the armor and chose the potency of vulnerability?*

➢ *Would disease disappear?*

➢ *Would conflict ease?*

➢ *Would you be happy?*

➢ *How would the energy of expansion open you up to a world of new possibilities?*

There is a life beyond abuse... beyond a cage that keeps you small and impotent.

You don't have to be young, as I was at seven staring at the moon, dreaming of a life beyond abuse, to begin to use the tremendous pull of the energy of expansion. It works for everyone no matter where you are.

All that's required is for you to choose to play with it, and that's what the next chapter is all about.

Seven

Playing with the Light

Every day you play with the light of the universe.
~ Pablo Neruda

Life can be much simpler – and way more fun – than most of us make it out to be.

So simple in fact that, for the most part, my entire 25 years of working in non-traditional and energetic therapies boils down to one major theme: Find out what's not working for people, empower a better choice, contribute to the actualization of their desire and generate the multiple possibilities of creating their desired life.

When I be this, the results are stunning.

And it isn't just that they're happier, though they are that. It's also that whatever the "issue" is – as indicated by the medications they're on, the diseases they have, the lack of money, or something else – also goes away. Poof! Like magic... and all that's required for achieving these results is the willingness to choose for yourself and bring the energy and demand of play into your life. So why aren't more people doing it?

That's a very good question....

What I've found in my work is that most people with a history of abuse have a difficult time playing, having fun, and letting go. It's not that they don't have the ability – we all do – it's that play, in their minds, has become associated with something entirely different – and "bad."

For example, sometimes play turned into sexual activity where something feels wrong but good at the same time. It's confusing because you're not really sure what's wrong, what's right, or what's going on. In this scenario, play becomes associated with sexual shame, a sense of wrongness that says, "I shouldn't be doing this," and anything that resembles it – fun, looseness, lightness – equates to feeling out of control, similar to what you felt like when you were being abused.

In real play, you're engaging in an activity for enjoyment and recreation, inviting something new to exist through imagination, activity, possibility, generation and creation.

With abuse, play changes. It becomes serious and practical, all about "what's going to happen," which then constricts – cutting off the freedom and awareness to just frolic, like a child running around free.

When you're a child, you don't have thoughts that worry and wonder if something bad is going to happen again. Few things are more fun than the element of the unknown, the anticipation, the surprise. What child hasn't eagerly asked the question, "Did you bring me a surprise?" and clapped their hands with delight and expectation? On the other hand, to someone who has an abusive past, surprise is the last thing they want. Hypervigilance becomes the watchword. And looking behind your back or around the corner becomes the game of survival.

The Robber Baron of Play

With abuse, you get locked down in having to hold your body a certain way, constricting yourself a certain way, doing things a certain way so you don't encounter abuse again. You go into the energy of conclusion, decision, judgement, and restriction. Like a bad case of arthritis, you become so rigid that you walk yourself out of any creativity, generation, and fluidity. You're stuck in what I call the invisible cage of abuse, which I describe fully in my next book, *Kick Abuse in the Caboose.*

In this self-imposed cage, you can't have any fun because you're always waiting for the next catastrophe to occur. Navigating life becomes somewhat like rafting through white water rapids. In this state, you wonder, "Why does this keep happening to me? Everything is such a struggle. Nothing ever works for me no matter how hard I try. Why is everything so hard?"

The answer is that, essentially, you're locked in the four "pillars," or the four "D's" – introduced in Chapter Three – that make up the invisible cage: Denying, Defending, Disconnecting, and Dissociating.

In this stance towards life, even the simplest creative activities, such as hiking by yourself can be rendered off limits because you're too acutely aware of yourself in a world that has become a dangerous place. Constantly on guard, aware that at any time your safety or comfort can be interrupted, it spreads to other aspects of your being. It's everywhere – in your body, relationships, money, sexualness – constricting and contracting instead of expanding into new possibility.

From a health standpoint, rigidity and lockdown in your body can have serious repercussions. Without a fluid, free-flowing form, blockage can ensue, literally constricting the blood flow, depriving your organs of oxygen and other vital elements your body requires to function effortlessly. Over time, this can further deteriorate into chronic conditions or possibly adrenal or endocrine disorders easily. It certainly did for me.

With relationships, you may tend to choose people who are more indicative of the lockdown that's present and stuck in your body because that's how you know, or think, relationships should be. You energetically choose people, consciously or unconsciously, that constrict you rather than those who create possibility for and with you. Even your income and potential to earn money is at risk because of your need to play it safe. An example would be taking a job you don't really like but that gives you a salary you can count on, even though you hate going to it every day. Where's the fun in that choice?

It's like living backwards, against the energy instead of moving forward with possibility. Life becomes "How safe am I?" instead of "How amazing! What else can I create?"

Play and creativity are fueled with imagination, a mind that is open and questioning, a relaxed space, and the possibility of something generative and expansive occurring. These are quite the opposite of what happens when your mind is held captive in the invisible cage of abuse:

- ➤ High need for structure
- ➤ Controlling
- ➤ Prepared for anything
- ➤ Need to know it all
- ➤ Withdrawn and isolated
- ➤ Conclusion oriented
- ➤ Conforming
- ➤ Mistrust of the unknown
- ➤ Unsafe
- ➤ Hypervigilant awareness

Your creative forces are kept flowing by tapping into the molecular energetics of the freewheeling knowingness of pure possibility – one where anything is possible and communion is the source of creation.

In play, there are a lot of unknowns and how does it get any better than that? You get to create everything and anything you desire. Yet, if you experienced any form of abuse, that "unknown" quality could trigger fear and destroy creation.

RADICAL AND ORGASMIC ALIVENESS

Have you ever noticed how long children stay with something? They just move from one thing to the next thing – mind and body together – fully present in the moment. They choose their next moment based on what's fun and exciting.

In my work, I refer to this as full radical and orgasmic aliveness, where your whole being is present with everything that you're doing. You're not worrying about the future, paying your bills, or how you look, and there's a great sense of fun and play in just being present.

With abusive situations, you don't want to be there at all.

Orgasm isn't just about sex... it's about sensual, embodied pleasure. What if you want to smell a rose, or buy roses for yourself to have beautiful color in your house? What if you want to put strawberries on your granola and just the taste of it is was orgasmic and delicious? That's fun and orgasmic! Kids don't have preconceived ideas; they haven't developed the notions that we've learned as adults that constrict us and keep us from embodying full pleasure.

And, if you don't want to be in your body, how do you think that affects, say, a relationship that is sexual and sensual? It's hard to have a desirable and orgasmic sexual relationship when you're so used to abandoning your body in order to not feel what you didn't want in the first place.

What, then, can you do to bring yourself fully into your body...and fully into play?

Two Steps into Play

When you were growing up, were you ever told to ask yourself, "Am I having fun right now?" For most adults, choosing for the fun of it is a foreign concept, hardly a choice at all. If you've never been in your body, you've also probably never given yourself the choice to ask and demand for yourself. Would you even know what question to ask?

The first step to play is to simply become aware that something isn't working for you and give yourself the allowance to say, "I don't really know what's going on here, but something doesn't feel right and I choose to make a change, even if I don't know what to ask." Just that awareness will bring you present to yourself.

The next step is to ask questions that invoke the energy of play such as:

- ➤ *Body, is this fun for me?*
- ➤ *Am I having fun right now?*
- ➤ *Am I learning something?*
- ➤ *Is this expanding my reality?*
- ➤ *Am I grateful?*
- ➤ *Am I enjoying what I'm being right now?*
- ➤ *Is this person receiving me?*
- ➤ *Am I able to receive?*
- ➤ *Does my body feel good?*
- ➤ *What else is possible here?*

> ➢ *Can I do whatever I want?*
> ➢ *Am I living my fun-filled, play-filled reality?*
> ➢ *What else could I choose that would be more playful?*

The energy of play isn't about doing what was fun as a kid – it's the spirit of fun and the playground of possibility you had then in the now. It's about what can you do to create a new possibility and get out of the constriction every day.

For example, I could sit in front of my computer all day mailing things out and responding to people, but that's not really fun for me. What's more fun is doing the energy work, the Voice of America radio show, writing these chapters, and talking with people, creating possibility. But there was a long time in my own life where play became unsafe, and I was more rigid and better with form and structure. If anything upset that, I'd get freaked out. Now I barely have a structure. I just go with the energy of "what is" and what is required of me each day.

This is what we do as kids. We just go with the energy of what's possible today. When abuse occurs, innocent freedom and your playground of possibility gets all locked up, limited, and constricted. Fortunately, there is a way back.

Light is Right

What's fun for people is what's light for them; it's something you can feel in your body. Lightness is like the truth – because the most expansive, joyful thing you like doing lightens everyone. You're more fun for all of us.

The energy of play is about discovering what your fun reality is – emotionally, financially, relationally, sexually, and otherwise – by asking, "Body, what would you like to do today? Who would you like to be with? Who would you like to sleep with? What would you like to eat? What would you like to create? What part of your business requires your attention today?"

If my body tells me, "Let's go to the gym," and I don't go, it gets really unhappy. Going to the gym can be a form of play, moving the spirit and energy. Or if it says, "Eat this," and I eat something else, I'm overriding it. The whole idea is to listen to your body, to the whispers your body is telling you about what it requires each day – and what you require each day – and going forward with it.

You can bring this energy of play into all your decisions of what's right for you. How? Well, what's fun for you? Do that!

What's Fun for You Is Play!

This is what makes you work through the day without eating, then suddenly look up and think, "Oh, wow, I haven't eaten!" You're having fun because you're really into what you're doing. You're living off the energy just as children do, who continually need reminding, "You have to eat now... you've got to go to bed now." They're in the moment with a freedom you have to walk them out of.

Usually adults have to relearn what light or heavy feels like so that, when presented with choice, they know it in their body. Where there's been abuse, your energy is infiltrated, your space is violated, and your consciousness is anesthetized. With all of that happening, how could you know what's light and right for you? You only know what is suffering and bad for you. Abuse takes your whole view of life and twists it to be more dangerous and not so fun.

Becoming aware of what's light and right for you allows you to create what's fun for you. It's like redefining your molecules to what they knew before they were abused. If it feels light and expansive and bubbly, go for it. If it's heavy and dense, ask more questions and don't choose it until lightness exists. Unfortunately, too many of us choose the heavy and dense and not the light, and that's how we wake up in psychiatry offices waiting for medication.

Just remember...

What's light is right.

The fun is in being a demand for yourself, like children who just go with, "Hey, let's do this!" and, "Hey, let's do that!" Of course, as adults, there's a little more pragmatic nature to it, but if you embody the energy of play I'm talking about here, you'll engage your generative, creative imagination. It's the childlike innocence that's in all of us, which lives within our bodies no matter what age we are.

And it's as easy as choosing to be fully present doing what works for you – right now – in the most light and expansive way.

10-SECOND INCREMENTS

Especially when starting out, the "Light and Heavy" tool is particularly effective when you do it combined with choosing in 10-second increments. This means you make a choice 10 seconds at time, giving yourself the freedom to change your mind and tuning in to what is most true for you in any moment. That's play.

The beauty of 10 seconds is two-fold: 1) you tap into more freedom and 2) discover more intimacy with yourself. If you choose something and it doesn't work for you, then in the next 10 seconds you choose again. Each choice gives you an awareness of what works for you, keeping in mind that what worked for you yesterday may not work for you next week, or what worked for you an hour ago may not work for you now.

If you've never lived in 10-second increments, as you can imagine, you go back and forth between freedom and constriction pretty regularly. But, we're only looking for one degree of shift to make a change. Like a muscle, you build on it.

Sometimes I'm asked how purpose figures into this. Well, if you're choosing in 10-second increments, you can't really get locked into much of a purpose. It's more about pleasure, knowing that living a joyous, playful life creates happiness – and I would propose that happiness and consciousness are the biggest targets we have on this planet.

Think about how many happy people you know. Have you ever noticed that everything seems to come to them with ease, joy and glory™?

When I'm happy, everything works. When I'm in my play-filled energy, I only focus on expansion and possibility. I'm just here enjoying every moment on this planet as a new possibility of generation and creation for a brand new reality – one that breeds joy, pleasure, possibility, play, and happiness. That's quite a different reality than someone who's been abused and thinks, "Everything's so hard and, no matter how much I do or hard I try, nothing ever changes for me."

PLAY IS PRAGMATIC

...find what is most interesting to you. The more you learn, the more you want to learn. It is fun.
~ Warren Buffett

The energy of play isn't only fun – it's also pragmatic. It's certainly worked for Warren Buffett who, in Tap Dancing to Work by Carol

Loomis, is described as motivated by having fun, not making money. And I've had many clients leave jobs for something they really love and, when they do, make three or four times the amount they did before.

When your body tells you what it wants and you do it, what shows up in your life becomes more easy and fun-filled. By listening to what's right for you and bringing that forward, you're conspiring with the universe to make your life easier – all because you're doing what's fun for you.

Conversely, if something's not working for you, you eliminate it from your reality. This doesn't mean not paying your bills, but rather finding another, more fun and joyous way to take care of things.

For example, I have my bills on an automatic payment plan with my bank because it's not fun for me to spend time figuring it out each month. Knowing it's handled every day, every month – that's fun for me and when I have created beyond the payments I pay it off. I like never having to worry about being late with anything; that's not where I desire to put my attention. I'd rather put it on creating a new possibility and, if that's something beyond what I currently have, I know I have free choice to go and create the extra money for it.

The Bridge to Radical Aliveness

As the catalyst of the Live Your ROAR movement, the target is to eradicate all forms of abuse off this planet through two overarching methods: identifying the invisible cage of abuse and directing people to cross the "bridge" to radical aliveness.

Remember, Radical Aliveness is made up of the four components, or "4 C's": Choosing for you, Committing to you, Collaborating and knowing that the universe is conspiring to bless you, and Creating the life you desire.

Radical Aliveness is fun!

You cross this bridge when you enter into the spirit of play and choose what's fun for you. The whole goal in the energy of play is to put yourself first.

If you're not used to doing this, then the idea of choosing for you is going to be a radically new perspective. For sure, people who have been abused are the most confounded by this notion because they put everybody else first – they don't exist.

Play acts to reclaim your freedom of expression.

Beyond intentions and goals, learning to choose for you from the energy of play will open you to possibility in every moment, and bring you back into communion with all life at a whole new level of ease, joy and glory.

In the next chapter, I'll introduce you to the energy of spirit and knowing – an intrinsic, unconscious part of all children that, abuse or not, tends to get dropped and left behind on the road to adulthood.

Because, as you will see, the more you make friends with this innate energy and use it, the easier it is to enter into the spirit of play.

Eight

THE FACE IN THE MOON

*I ended up falling in love with the moon because it faithfully
showed up night after night.*
~ Unknown

My room was my sanctuary when I was a child growing up in an
extremely violent and abusive household. It was the only place I could
get away from all the craziness in my house. There was a little window
by my bed, and every night when the moon would come out, I would
get on my knees and stare at it for hours, basking in the beautiful face
looking back at me, feeling its smiling energy, letting me know that
everything was okay.

One night, after one of my long dialogues with the moon, I remember turning around and seeing that my entire room had turned into all
the colors of the rainbow with fairies and angels, what I now know as
gods and goddesses, entities and deities, dancing around in a wild party—the pink light of compassion, the blue light of creativity—all there
for me to experience.

I began spending time in that special world of magical energies and received all kinds of downloads about what to be aware of, the gifts I possessed and how special and different I was to be in this life. These otherworldly creatures became my friends and playmates, and some nights I couldn't wait to go to my room. I had always known something else was available so I wasn't scared of this realm, and it made more sense to me than my current reality, even though it defied ordinary time and space.

What I realized was that something else was possible and that none of the insanity could affect me when I was in that energy. It was then that I knew my life's work was to bridge the spirit world with the physical world and tap into the ATP energy of creation. ATP (adenosine triphosphate), or spirit energy as I call it, provides us with the energy of everything and it is in every cell of our body... including that of the universe and the earth we live upon.

THE ENERGY OF SPIRIT AND KNOWING

What is this energy that we can all call upon and commune with? What is this spirit that moves through all things...that creates all things?

Today, when I think of spirit, I don't think of fairies or angels or entities. Instead, I think of something Amma (a spiritual healer I spent 15 years with as part of a spiritual community) would say – the child-like energy deep within us is God.

The energy of spirit is, to me, like the ATP (adenosine triphosphate) molecule which fuels every cell in our body and is literally called the energy currency of life. It's the spirit energy that's in our bodies and what we all are.

There was a time in my life when I was really unhappy, I was drinking a lot, depressed and heavy, and nothing was working out. I felt terrible and very alone inside, like everything was going on around me and I wasn't connected to anything.

One night I was drinking and decided to check out and just be done. It wasn't premeditated, but when I saw a bus approaching, I stepped off the curb to stand right in front of it, and felt something grab my shoulders and pull me back. I was in shock. I looked around and there was nothing or no one there, and that's when I knew that somebody or something had my back. It was the wake-up call I so badly needed to remind me that there's something way beyond this reality and it's connected to me and I needed to find out more about this. And there have been so many times I have felt held in my journey and guided to where I am now.

After I'd become a psychotherapist and started my business, I got sick with a life-threatening disease and, to heal myself, began to use Theta Healing®. It completely changed my practice. With this technique, you really have to work on your knowing of spirit. Every day, I would sit in my office chair with clients and I would, as Sheryl Sandberg, COO of Facebook and author of best seller, *Lean In*, says, "lean in" to listen to the energy of spirit, the energy of knowing.

I would come up with information I had no conscious way of knowing, and my clients would often look at me somewhat shocked. They'd demand, "How did you know that? How could you know that? Where did you get that information? I didn't tell you that." And I would have to be gentle with my knowing so as to not overwhelm them with what I was able to tap into through the energy of spirit.

At that time, I'd use tools like muscle testing and, later, in Access Consciousness®, 'light and heavy' to help my clients feel their own knowing through their body and to empower them to know what they know. It became very clear to me that I was being a channel, a hollow reed (everything comes through me and is for you with no judgement or point of view), for the people that came into my office because of the connection to these other realms, realities, and energies.

And even before Theta Healing®, I'd always had the sense that there was another part of me connecting with people that was unique and unusual. I knew it and my clients knew it. They'd say things like, "You're a different counselor than I've ever had before. You do this differently. I've never felt this way before."

I believe I have this capacity because of my awareness of the energy of the 'face in the moon,' my awareness of the energy that moves in all things, including our belief systems, and my awareness that the organs in our body store those beliefs, which in turn form our bodies and all our realities. I also believe these realities can be changed, transformed, and healed by collaborating with the awareness of something beyond this reality.

To be aware in this way is to collaborate with the earth and to collaborate with the molecules inherent in the earth, which are no different than the molecules of our body that hold the ATP, the powerhouse of our body.

Because of this early experience with the spirit of energy and knowing, and the information I received, I've always felt that my work in the world was to bridge these two worlds—the spirit with the physical. It's probably no accident that I'm Sagittarius, represented by the Archer and depicted as both a human archer shooting toward the sky and a horse grounded in the earth. I'm that bridge for people between our current reality and what else is possible in other realms.

With any client I work with, myself included, I'm looking for the parts of us that fragmented off, blocking our ability to access our own knowing and our energy of spirit. It can mean going back to a very young age and tracing back to where they are still stuck in some scene at whatever age that scene took place. I help them look directly into the eye of their inner child to get the information about whatever is keeping them stuck and cut off from themselves and explore the emotion that is there – the fear, the rage, the shame – and then acknowledge it with the adult them.

It's all done eye to eye.

Once they've said everything that needs to be said in that moment, I always ask them, as the adult, to reach out their hand to the child. Sometimes they'll take it and sometimes they won't, but eventually we work it so the child will, either in that session or another one. Usually the child will ask, "Can I trust you?" Essentially, it has to "meet" the adult. To me, this is like meeting our own energy of spirit or inner ally. This is true communion of spirit.

When they're returning from this scene, there's usually a rainbow escalator carrying both the child in the scene and the adult back to the office where we are, or the group, and we integrate that child into the now. It never fails that the adult says this experience has fundamentally changed them. They're no longer triggered by things that used to bother them, as witnessed by this excerpt from a testimonial I received from one of my clients:

> *I have tried so many things to change all the aspects in my life that have not been working. I have been so incredibly frustrated and often near giving up, taking class after class, using tools that were given to me, knowing they should be working as dynamically as they seem to work with other people, but not knowing why they did not work for me. I have worked with many, many facilitators, some of whom have succeeded in assisting me to the edge of looking into the trauma and abuse, only to be left hanging once the door to the abuse was opened because the facilitator really did not know what was required once that*

*door was opened. This was terrible for me and it took a long time
to even be willing to try again...*

*As I left the class to go home, I noticed that instead of the shal-
low breathing I have lived with all my life, my breath reached all
the way inside my body, as if I was finally living in my body for
the first time. My body feels totally different. My being feels more
connected to my body and everything is softer. I am so grateful
that you provided the space; that you brought all of your amazing skills to bear on helping me get reconnected with myself. I
know that things will never be the same and I know now that the
gift that I am is available to me in every moment.*

This is the energy of spirit, and that's what I'm doing. I'm calling
up these lost children – the fragmented spirits of these amazing be-
ings – and connecting them to "the childlike innocence deep within
us which is God," bringing them forward, allowing this human being
to have full choice, full power, and full capacity in every moment to
collaborate with everything.

Without this energy of spirit and knowing, you feel like you have
a manual with all the parts and pieces missing. You can't perceive the
wholeness of the spirit because of the separation that's taken place.

In this work, before I can even get to the child, though, I have to
clear the judgements, beliefs and embodiments that the person before
me – the adult – thinks is them. When the body is empty of beliefs
and judgements that aren't theirs in the first place, such as parents',
grandparents', cultural belief systems, vows, and/or obligations, this is
when I often find children who are stuck in scenes where they didn't
know what to do. A psychologically compensatory mechanism kicks
in when a part of us leaves and another part stays stuck in the scene at
four years of age. That part doesn't die or leave the scene, it stays stuck

in the kitchen or the bedroom or wherever the scene was.

There are all kinds of scenes where this can happen. It might have simply been a mother and father screaming at each other and one of them threatening to leave. But what the child hears is, "Oh my god, my whole safety is threatened." They can't deal with that or talk about it, so they separate themselves and hide in the closet in their bedroom.

Forty years later, they're in therapy and that scene is at the heart of the issue.

Fortunately, they don't have to stay stuck, and this is part of what my work is about. I go and retrieve that part with them after we release and acknowledge whatever it was that created the separation, as well as whatever it was they took on from that separation that isn't true. This has been the problem – they're not creating their life from the wholeness of who they really are. They're making it from a part of them created in trauma and in shock.

When we bring that other part back, they feel what my client felt – that everything has changed and nothing will be the same again. They now have a connection with their own spirit, their own energy, their own infinite being-ness, which is phenomenal and magical, and they are filled with possibilities and full choice no matter how bad it gets. It's no longer a no-choice universe.

There's another possibility.

How do we connect to the wholeness of spirit?

Connecting to Wholeness

The energy of spirit is that part we call by many names – God or the universe, infinite knowing, it doesn't matter – it is that which we perceive as something distinct that gifts us and works in collaboration with us. The energy of knowing is internal; it's our ability to receive intuition; our perceiving, knowing and being.

To become more aware of these energies, there are practices or ideas outside of therapy or classes – steps you can take on a personal level to connect with your innate wholeness:

Get Out in Nature

One of the things that held me while exploring my path to spirit was my participation in sports. When I was playing soccer, hiking, biking, running up the top of a mountain, I felt strong, agile, and free in my body and the knowing I could do anything. There were no limits to my agility and ability to commune with my body and the earth. I felt a peace after being active that breathed, "Everything is okay."

When you're in that energy of space, anything is possible and you can expand out with the universe and be one with all the molecules. Basically, it's about having gratitude for the earth by getting out on to the earth somehow.

So, go ahead...hug a tree. Take a barefoot meditation walk. Put your body and being closer to the earth and breathe in.

My Beloved Grandmother - The Art of Receiving

My grandmother opened up space in my world to receive the energy of being me more completely.

When I was a young child, the only person I felt good with was my grandmother. I used to walk my grandmother to church each day when I stayed with her, and she would recite the prayers in the church pew.

One day she recited, "Someday my soul and I shall be healed." Now the prayer book actually didn't say "soul," but she added it, and when I heard the word "soul" I immediately looked up at her and heard a ringing in my ears like, "What's the soul?"

Looking back, I realize my whole entire life has been on a quest for soul and spirit, which was first opened up by those long ago introductory experiences with the moon.

Listening to the chants, prayers, and psalms over and over again, while sitting at my grandmother's feet and tracing the veins on her hands, over and over, I felt so comforted by the repetition of her words. Through her 'religion,' I opened to my awareness, my perceiving, my knowing and that afforded me the luxury of being. We all require at least one person, in addition to ourselves, that somehow reflects to us the brilliance we be. Those moments infuse our knowing beyond this reality. From there we choose communion intrinsically.

Ask

If you recall, in Chapter Two I talked about the importance of asking questions as a way to collaborate with the Universe. Asking and being in the question is an inherent part of connecting with your knowing. It can be as simple as asking for the next step in your life or what you really want.

Something that I've found works in my own life to connect me with the energy of spirit and knowing is focusing on what my target is by asking a series of questions and phrases. I actually sing it in a song each morning starting out:

> ➤ *Who am I today?*
> ➤ *What grand and glorious adventure awaits me?*
> ➤ *What else is possible®?*
> ➤ *How does it get any better than this®?*
> ➤ *Universe, show me something beautiful today.*

- *What energy, space and consciousness can I create in myself?*
- *What contribution from spirit/knowing can I be and receive today?*

I also add something fun like, "What can I do or be today that will create more play, fun and joy right away?"

Sometimes I ask my business things like:

- *What would it take for me to out-create myself financially today?*
- *What does my business require of me?*
- *What would it like to do today?*
- *Who do I need to speak to today?*

For my health I might ask:

- *How would my body like to move today?*
- *How would my body like to eat today that fills me with energy and lightness?*

I have to thank Access Consciousness and the founders, Gary Douglas and Dr. Dain Heer, for their contribution to the 'song of my spirit' by way of questions that keeps me fresh and alive in possibility every day.

It's Okay to Let Go

Sometimes you have to let go of something that's not working and say, "Okay, I give in to what is way beyond me." In a way, the entire creating process is one big let go – letting go of attachment to something you desire. Expectation, decision, judgment, conclusion and projections can disregard your knowing, perceiving and receiving ability.

What I know to be true is that we live in a universe that conspires to bless us. No matter how much abuse I suffered or how much I didn't want to live at times, the energy of my knowing was what kept me going and what kept me navigating those tortuous waters to come out on the other side and be able to offer something valuable to help so many others.

Many people are lost in this reality and look for therapy, meditation, or spiritual communities to connect with all the energy I saw so clearly at the age of seven. I've done those things, too, in an effort to heal and connect more deeply.

So, here's what I'm wondering...

It's a question, a call for action, if you will.

If you can expand your energy to include working with the spirit of the earth, the Universe, and your own knowingness to collaborate with them all, what else can we create together so that we be the energy of spirit at all times, in all places, in every situation whether we feel completely supported or not?

And what would it take for the energy of spirit from deep within you to show up and be the catalyst in your life for now and all eternity?

After all, the world *is* waiting for you.

In the following chapter, I'll share some steps, along with some simple yet powerful tips, that you can put into practice today in support of experiencing true happiness in your own life. I've shared these steps with thousands of my clients.

Believe me, they work.

Nine

THE KEY TO HAPPINESS RESTS INSIDE OF YOU

You can run, run, run away from lots of things in life,
but you can't run away from yourself. And the key to happiness
is to understand and accept who you are.
~ Dale Archer

There were many steps I took after that fateful day in college when my professor reached out to me. It's not like happiness came to me overnight. As I've shared, I had to overcome two decades of abuse so that I can honestly say I am truly happy. I feel joyful, light, and free.

And you can, too.

Whether or not you've struggled with abuse, chances are, if you're reading this book, there's something in your life that feels like a trap, a cage, some way you feel locked out of the possibility of happiness. The good news is that the key to this cage rests inside of you and I can help you find it and use it.

STEP 1: ACKNOWLEDGE YOUR UNHAPPINESS

Happiness is seeing all of you.

Ignoring unhappiness doesn't make it go away. In fact, ignoring it ensures that it will stick around a whole lot longer than you want it to. It's like a troublesome guest at a party: ignore it and it will create a ruckus!

You may deny you're unhappy because you're embarrassed or even ashamed to admit to others just how unhappy you are. You aren't alone in this. I was horrified to admit my unhappiness to others.

Yet when you deny your unhappiness, you're telling yourself you don't matter. *This is actually a form of neglect and abuse.* Imagine this part of you that feels so unhappy being left alone in a closet, in the dark. Would you do this to a little child? Then don't do this to yourself.

When you acknowledge your unhappiness, you value your experience; you value yourself. You let yourself know, "Hey, I matter." This opens up a whole new realm of possibilities for what you can be or do from here.

This also helps you begin to build a bridge between your mind and your body. Rather than leaving that unhappy part of you behind in a closet, all of you is engaged and available. This sets you up for success.

STEP 2: CHOOSE HAPPINESS

Happiness is choosing just for the fun of it.

In my early 20s, I didn't think life was ever going to get any better. I didn't believe I would ever be happy. I thought happiness was only available to others. When I graduated college I knew I couldn't return to the house I grew up in. I knew that would kill me, yet I wasn't sure what I wanted to do.

Inspired by my college professor, I decided to move to Arizona and work at a Youth Crisis Shelter. I chose to be in an environment where I knew I could make a difference. Through the shelter, I worked with Child Protective Services to provide safe housing, education and meals for children who were removed from violent homes. I also got to counsel these children. I wanted every child to know they were safe, loved and cared for. I wanted them to be able to lay their head on the pillow at night without any worries or fears.

Helping these children gave me happiness.

As I was an ally for them, I became an ally for myself. As I gave myself the love and care I never had growing up, I discovered I could make different choices for myself.

All those painful ways I had been living and relating previously slowly began to fade as I chose differently. For example, rather than trying to escape by drinking or snorting, I could choose activities that felt good. I made choices based on what I *now* wanted to be and do, not what I'd been doing.

I could actually choose happiness.

You have a choice, too. In the same way, you can choose happiness by bringing something into your life that's fun, that lights you up and brings you happiness.

What is this for you? A hobby? Going to the gym? Taking a dance class? Volunteering? What's the thing in the back of your mind that makes no sense to do, yet you know would bring you happiness? It may be something you did as a child, or it may be something you've never done before or imagined you would do. Whatever it is, it could be the doorway to your happiness.

Choose it.

Choose happiness.

Step 3: Release Your Addiction to Unhappiness

Happiness is allowing ease.

Unfortunately, a lot of people are addicted to their unhappiness. This sounds crazy, right? Why would someone *choose* unhappiness?

Well, as it turns out, there can be many motivations:

- ✓ It's familiar.
- ✓ It's a way to get attention.
- ✓ It's a way to connect (complaining about what's not working in life is one way this society forms relationships).

When things aren't working, people take you out to coffee; they take you shopping; or they suggest a spa day.

Yet when things are going really well, some people get mad at you or wonder what drug you're on. They aren't called to support you or to take you out. *In fact, others often don't know how to relate to someone's joy and success.*

Unhappiness has become a habit. Pessimism pervades. Our lives are fueled by the struggle of what's not working. Yet what if you didn't need to struggle to come out of unhappiness?

Addictions are a dis-ease.

Happiness is ease.

People with addictions to alcohol struggle to release their habit. Ultimately, to truly surrender their grip on the bottle, they need support.

Similarly, unhappiness is an addiction, too. In order to release your grip on this disease, stop thinking you can do it all on your own. Be willing to ask for support.

STEP 4: GET SUPPORT AND SHARE YOUR STORY

Happiness is receiving you as a gift.

I tried to overcome my own trauma and unhappiness on my own, yet that didn't get me anywhere. I turned to drinking and drugs to numb out for a while because I couldn't stand the pain I was in.

I finally had to admit to myself that I needed support, so I read every self-help book I could find. They gave me insights into healing and happiness, yet they weren't enough.

It was my professor at college who offered the support I needed by providing a safe place for me to share my story. Until this time, all my secrets and worries had been locked inside my body, neglected and abandoned.

How can you experience true happiness with parts of you locked up?

In order to stop choosing unhappiness and start choosing happiness, you need to delve into the root of your unhappiness. This requires looking at events, situations and relationships in your past that are impacting your present.

The heaviness of your unhappiness is lifted when you have the eyes and ears of a professional, whether it's a therapist, doctor, or other practitioner. Sharing your story in this way begins to unlock you from the cage of unhappiness.

When you do this you move from enslavement to freedom, from limitation to possibility. You can't create a new present and future until you face the past that led you to where you are. You need to share your story, learn from it, and discover how you can create a new one.

Once you enlist the support of a trusted advisor, you'll feel a profound sense of relief that you no longer need to struggle on your own.

Step 5: Learn to Listen Within

Happiness is getting quiet, listening, and doing exactly what you hear.

It may seem odd that first I encourage you to get support and then

I tell you to listen to your own guidance, yet both are important. Working with a therapist helps you clear away a lot of your inner 'static' so you can tune in and listen to your own inner guidance. Ultimately, it's your inner guidance that's actually the key to your happiness.

Many people make the mistake of thinking they'll be happy when they have the BMW, the corporate job, the marriage to the "right person," the white-picket fence and the 2.5 kids.

But here's the truth...

Creating a life based on what you think you're supposed to have, or based on what others have, is the ticket to unhappiness. It causes you to make decisions from the outside in, rather than from the inside out.

When you take time to tune into your inner voice and allow that wisdom to guide your decisions, you begin to make different choices. You also begin creating a new relationship with yourself based on trust and respect. This goes a long way in cultivating happiness for yourself and with others.

Most likely you've spent most of your life listening to others' voices, so it may take some time to tune in and listen to your own inner voice.

The following is a practice you can do daily to strengthen your ability to hear your inner voice:

a. Set a timer for (at least) 5 minutes.
b. Ask yourself these questions:
   What do I want?
   What experience am I looking for?
   What will help me get that?
c. Listen for and write down the answers to each one. (Don't try to "figure out" the answers just let yourself write in a

stream of consciousness way without editing or stopping.)

When you listen to and act on your inner guidance, you're living from the inside out. This is your ticket to true happiness.

Step 6: Weed Out and Plant New Seeds

Happiness is allowing yourself to plant your own garden.

To be blunt, if you want to be happy, you need to be willing to question everything in your life. You need to be willing to change *anything* that's not contributing to your choice to be happy.

Being happy is an "inside job." However, the people, events, and situations you surround yourself with either add to or detract from your happiness.

How willing are you to acknowledge that something you've been doing for "X" number of years is no longer fulfilling – and how often do you avoid changing it?

You can't be happy without pulling out some of the weeds that have clogged up your life, so once you've acknowledged that something isn't working for you:

Thank it for all that it has given you.
Release it with love and gratitude, without conflict.

Now that you've pulled the weeds out, there's space for planting new seeds. You get to ask, "What's going to make me happy?"

Everything you've done for these steps will support you with planting new seeds of happiness. And just like any gardener tends her plants on a regular basis, you, too, need to regularly cultivate the garden of your life by weeding and tending to the new seeds you plant.

STEP 7: UNLEASH YOUR AWESOME

Happiness is leaping into the unknown and knowing the net will appear.

Now it gets really good – even better than good.

It gets awesome!

As you take Steps 1 through 6, you begin to create a life for yourself beyond all your familiar reference points. There are no longer any limitations to what you can be or do. You become the creator of all new possibilities.

This is when you "Unleash Your Awesome" and leap into more happiness than you ever thought possible.

And here's where it gets tricky...

You may start to doubt and question yourself, "Can I really have all of this?" (Remember Step 3 and the addiction to unhappiness?) Or you may be afraid to make the leap.

"Will there be a net?"

"Will I fall flat on my face?"

When this happens, it's up to you to choose again.

"Do I choose to believe the Universe is against me or supporting me?"

I believe in the air even though I can't see it. It's not tangible and I can't hold it in my hand, yet I can't live without it. In the same way, you take the leap, knowing that the Universe has your back and a net will appear.

When you do, you'll be catapulted into the life you always dreamed possible. And the seeds you planted will blossom into more possibilities for you, too.

Keep in mind that you can't take this leap until you acknowledge you're unhappy, choose happiness, release your addiction to unhappiness, get support, listen, weed, and plant new seeds.

Now you're ready to unleash.

Much like the golden brick road, these steps are a solid recipe for happiness.

The real question is, will you choose?

Happiness is your divine birthright.

Afterword

Allow yourself to trust joy and embrace it.
You will find you dance with everything.
~ Ralph Waldo Emerson

If some of the ideas you've read seem like a radical perspective, it's to be expected.

When you've been living in a small way, controlling and portioning out your energy, confined within a tight circle of movement – in the *invisible cage of abuse* – it's bound to seem a bit fantastical, perhaps out of the realm of your imagination to do things completely differently...

To live a Radically Orgasmically Alive Reality.

Or, as I love to say it...

To live your *ROAR!*

The truth is, what I've presented here is only *just the start*, really, to get you going towards Radical Aliveness – sort of like 'Kick Abuse in the Caboose' on training wheels.

(If you would like to learn more, be sure to pick up a copy of *Kick*

Abuse in the Caboose when it's released, or visit my website at www. DrLisaCooney.com.)

Still, as I promised in the beginning, the tools – concepts, tips and steps – I've presented here will guide you through a morass of resistance that's been tethering you to a constricted experience of life.

Resistance comes in many forms – and most of them look quite 'real' and believable. It really appears that you don't have the money, time, energy, knowledge, or skill to do what you want.

But these aren't reasons or justifications.

They're *creations.*

And they all flow from the idea that "Something's wrong with me...see?"

If there's one thing to be said about resistance, it's that there's always *something* that stands between you and what you want. At the end of the day, though, they're all creations – disguised excuses – designed with one purpose in mind: to keep you from venturing out beyond what you know and perceive as safe.

When you look more closely, this kind of safety is a relative term, a moving target, that's defined by a context you created at some point to protect you. Yet when you live in an invisible cage of abuse created out of an abusive past, what is actually safe?

So the next time you feel resistance, afraid to face something, or feel like you've tried everything and nothing's working, here are a few questions to ask yourself:

If I knew this was stopping me, would I be willing to let it go?
Am I willing to let go of my judgement about this?
Am I willing to trade 'x' for 'y?'

In closing, true safety can only be experienced through expansion and consciousness, through your own awareness in the present. It comes from learning to recognize and listen to the whisperings of consciousness within you, trusting what you hear and acting on it moment by moment.

It's in choosing happiness and letting that be your guide.

It's *expanding* into the ease, lightness, joy, and fun that's possible when you choose for you.

And, ultimately, it's learning to live with kindness...

For others, for the planet, and most of all...

For *You.*

About the Author

Dr. Lisa Cooney is a creative, generative leader in the area of personal transformation and an expert on thriving beyond abuse. A licensed Marriage and Family Therapist, PhD., Master Theta Healer, and certified Access Consciousness® Facilitator, she's the creator of Live Your ROAR! Be You! Beyond Anything! Creating Magic! An internationally recognized expert, Dr. Lisa's work has allowed thousands of people to cross the bridge from childhood sexual abuse, and other forms of abuse, to living a "Radically Orgasmically Alive Reality" (ROAR).

The magic of her work centers on core concepts that she used to heal herself, not only from early childhood abuse, but from a life-threatening disease. These essential principles, which include the 4 C's – Choosing for you, Committing to you, Collaborating and knowing that the universe is conspiring to bless you, and Creating the life you desire – are the touchstone for deep and lasting transformation.

In addition to her own revolutionary and "revelatory" contributions to the body of transformative wisdom, she is gifted in using the creative tools of Access Consciousness and other modalities to facilitate others in moving beyond all obstacles and into a place of their own knowing...that space where they have direct access to the whisperings of consciousness.

Known for her "I'm Having It!... No Matter What!" approach to life, Dr. Lisa teaches people how to playfully engage this magical and generative energy to create a life that's light and right and fun for them.

Testimonials

Dr. Lisa Cooney is an amazing facilitator! She laser's in on what's going on and walks you through with nurturing support! She shines a bright light on what you hide in the crevices of you, that you do not know how to walk you way out of. I have had tons of change and new awareness of the reasons why I do what I do to me and people I care about. She gives me the tools to change even some of the deepest darkest traumas of my life. She has helped me uncover my beautiful true self. I NOW have TRUE CHOICE in my life to live freely as I choose! I highly recommend Dr.Lisa Cooney as a facilitator, body classes and living radically alive classes!!

> - SHERRI JORGENSEN

So much in my life has changed, from the first time I heard Dr.Lisa speak about creating and being Radical Aliveness Beyond Abuse. Not identifying with an abusive past, I have been surprised how much her wisdom can change anything... beyond abuse! My relationship with my body is different and better, and I am having more fun and being more present with my body than ever before. My relationships with others are easier and I am working with others in business, which is something I use to avoid. Most of all... I am choosing for me on a whole new level and creating a life that works for me. These are just a few of the ways Radical Aliveness is showing up for me, so far. How does it get better than that?

> ~ DONNA HILDEBRAND

Working with Dr. Lisa is the single best thing I have ever done for myself! My life has changed in ways I would have only dreamed of in the past. I have left behind a lifetime of living like a victim. In the process, I have become self-assured and healthier in every way – physically, mentally, emotionally and spiritually. I was able to leave a dreadful job, doubled my income and created a new business. I have lost more than a hundred pounds, and I have a healthy relationship with a loving partner. Thank you, thank you, thank you.

> ~ TRICIA

Dr. Lisa is such a powerful and committed healer, able to hold and transform every blockage presented to her. This created an atmosphere of deep trust and safety, enabling everyone's deepest fears, blockages and core beliefs to come up to the surface to be healed. It is an amazing gift to work with one of the world's most powerful healers.

~ STEPHEN

Lisa is the BEST! As a former gold medalist and world champion, I fully endorse the groundbreaking work that Dr. Lisa is doing in regard to individual empowerment and healing. IT WORKS!

~ PATRICK

The End

CPSIA information can be obtained
at www.ICGtesting.com
Printed in the USA
JSHW040047070721
16656JS00006B/150